Teaching the New English

Published in association with the English
Director: **Ben Knights**

Teaching the New English is an innovative series concerned with the teaching of the English degree in universities in the UK and elsewhere. The series addresses new and developing areas of the curriculum as well as more traditional areas that are reforming in new contexts. Although the series is grounded in intellectual and theoretical concepts of the curriculum, it is concerned with the practicalities of classroom teaching. The volumes will be invaluable for new and more experienced teachers alike.

Titles include:

Gail Ashton and Louise Sylvester (*editors*)
TEACHING CHAUCER

Charles Butler (*editor*)
TEACHING CHILDREN'S FICTION

Robert Eaglestone and Barry Langford (*editors*)
TEACHING HOLOCAUST LITERATURE AND FILM

Michael Hanrahan and Deborah L. Madsen (*editors*)
TEACHING, TECHNOLOGY, TEXTUALITY
Approaches to New Media

Andrew Hiscock and Lisa Hopkins (*editors*)
TEACHING SHAKESPEARE AND EARLY MODERN DRAMATISTS

Anna Powell and Andrew Smith (*editors*)
TEACHING THE GOTHIC

Forthcoming titles:

Gina Wisker (*editor*)
TEACHING AFRICAN-AMERICAN WOMEN'S WRITING

Teaching the New English
Series Standing Order ISBN 1–4039–4441–5 Hardback 1–4039–4442–3 Paperback
(*outside North America only*)

You can receive future titles in this series as they are published by placing a standing order. Please contact your bookseller or, in case of difficulty, write to us at the address below with your name and address, the title of the series and one of the ISBNs quoted above.

Customer Services Department, Macmillan Distribution Ltd, Houndmills, Basingstoke, Hampshire RG21 6XS, England

Also by Robert Eaglestone

ETHICAL CRITICISM: Reading after Levinas

DOING ENGLISH

POSTMODERNISM AND HOLOCAUST DENIAL

THE HOLOCAUST AND THE POSTMODERN

READING *THE LORD OF THE RINGS* (editor)

LEGACIES OF DERRIDA: Literature and Philosophy
(*co-editor with Simon Glendinning*)

Also by Barry Langford

FILM GENRE: Hollywood and Beyond

Teaching Holocaust Literature and Film

Edited by

Robert Eaglestone
Professor of Contemporary Literature and Thought
Royal Holloway, University of London

Barry Langford
Senior Lecturer in Film and Television Studies
Royal Holloway, University of London

Introduction, selection and editorial matter © Robert Eaglestone
and Barry Langford 2008
Individual chapters © contributors 2008

All rights reserved. No reproduction, copy or transmission of this
publication may be made without written permission.

No paragraph of this publication may be reproduced, copied or
transmitted save with written permission or in accordance
with the provisions of the Copyright, Designs and Patents Act 1988,
or under the terms of any licence permitting limited copying
issued by the Copyright Licensing Agency, 90
Tottenham Court Road, London W1T 4LP.

Any person who does any unauthorised act in relation to this
publication may be liable to criminal prosecution and
civil claims for damages.

The authors have asserted their rights to be identified as
the authors of this work in accordance with the Copyright,
Designs and Patents Act 1988.

First published in 2008 by
PALGRAVE MACMILLAN
Houndmills, Basingstoke, Hampshire RG21 6XS and
175 Fifth Avenue, New York, N.Y. 10010
Companies and representatives throughout the world.

PALGRAVE MACMILLAN is the global academic imprint of the Palgrave
Macmillan division of St. Martin's Press, LLC and of Palgrave
Macmillan Ltd. Macmillan® is a registered trademark in the United
States, United Kingdom and other countries. Palgrave is a registered
trademark in the European Union and other countries.

ISBN-13: 978–0–230–01936–2 hardback
ISBN-10: 0–230–01936–6 hardback
ISBN-13: 978–0–230–01937–9 paperback
ISBN-10: 0–230–01937–4 paperback

This book is printed on paper suitable for recycling and made from fully
managed and sustained forest sources. Logging, pulping and
manufacturing processes are expected to conform to the environmental
regulations of the country of origin.

A catalogue record for this book is available from the British Library.

A catalog record for this book is available from the Library of Congress.

10 9 8 7 6 5 4 3 2 1
17 16 15 14 13 12 11 10 09 08

Printed and bound in Great Britain by
CPI Antony Rowe, Chippenham and Eastbourne

Contents

Series Preface	vii
Notes on the Contributors	ix
Introduction Robert Eaglestone and Barry Langford	1
1 Issues Arising from Teaching Holocaust Film and Literature Sue Vice and Gwyneth Bodger	15
2 Holocaust Theory? Robert Eaglestone	28
3 The Role of Theories of Memory in Teaching Representations of the Holocaust Anne Whitehead	37
4 Teaching Holocaust Literature: Issues of Representation Nicola King	48
5 Mass Culture/Mass Media/Mass Death: Teaching Film, Television, and the Holocaust Barry Langford	63
6 "Representing the Holocaust": an Interdisciplinary Module Antony Rowland	78
7 Teaching the Holocaust in French Studies: Questions of Mediation and Experience Ursula Tidd	91
8 History, Memory, Fiction in French Cinema Libby Saxton	102
9 Teaching Primo Levi Rachel Falconer	114

10 Teaching Holocaust Literature and Film to History
   Students: Teaching *The Pawnbroker* (1961/1965)   126
   Tim Cole

11 *Sophie's Choice*: On the Pedagogical Value of the
   "Problem Text"   139
   R. Clifton Spargo

The Holocaust: Historical, Literary, and Cinematic Timeline   156

Further Reading   161

Index   167

Series Preface

One of many exciting achievements of the early years of the English Subject Centre was the agreement with Palgrave Macmillan to initiate the series "Teaching the New English." The intention of the then Director, Professor Philip Martin, was to create a series of short and accessible books which would take widely-taught curriculum fields (or, as in the case of learning technologies, approaches to the whole curriculum) and articulate the connections between scholarly knowledge and the demands of teaching.

Since its inception, "English" has been committed to what we know by the portmanteau phrase "learning and teaching." Yet, by and large, university teachers of English—in Britain at all events—find it hard to make their tacit pedagogic knowledge conscious, or to raise it to a level where it might be critiqued, shared, or developed. In the experience of the English Subject Centre, colleagues find it relatively easy to talk about curriculum and resources, but far harder to talk about the success or failure of seminars, how to vary forms of assessment, or to make imaginative use of Virtual Learning Environments. Too often this reticence means falling back on received assumptions about student learning, about teaching, or about forms of assessment. At the same time, colleagues are often suspicious of the insights and methods arising from generic educational research. The challenge for the English group of diciplines is therefore to articulate ways in which our own subject knowledge and ways of talking might themselves refresh debates about pedagogy. The implicit invitation of this series is to take fields of knowledge and survey them through a pedagogic lens. Research and scholarship, and teaching and learning are part of the same process, not two separate domains.

"Teachers," people used to say, "are born not made." There may, after all, be some tenuous truth in this: there may be generosities of spirit (or, alternatively, drives for didactic control) laid down in earliest childhood. But why should we assume that even "born" teachers (or novelists, or nurses, or veterinary surgeons) do not need to learn the skills of their trade? Amateurishness about teaching has far more to do with university claims to status, than with evidence about how people learn. There is a craft to shaping and promoting learning. This series of books is dedicated to the development of the craft of teaching within English Studies.

Ben Knights
Teaching the New English *Series Editor*
Director, English Subject Centre
Higher Education Academy

The English Subject Centre

Founded in 2000, the English Subject Centre (which is based at Royal Holloway, University of London) is part of the subject network of the Higher Education Academy. Its purpose is to develop learning and teaching across the English disciplines in UK Higher Education. To this end it engages in research and publication (web and print), hosts events and conferences, sponsors projects, and engages in day-to-day dialogue with its subject communities.

www.english.heacademy.ac.uk

Notes on the Contributors

Gwyneth Bodger is Affiliated Lecturer at the Centre for the Study of Jewish-Christian Relations, Cambridge. She has taught Holocaust Studies at undergraduate and postgraduate level, and also supervises research in this area. Her own research specializes in the area of testimony and trauma literature.

Tim Cole is Senior Lecturer in Social History at the University of Bristol. He is the author of *Images of the Holocaust/Selling the Holocaust* (1999) and *Holocaust City: the Making of a Jewish Ghetto* (2003) and is currently completing a book on the social history of the Holocaust in Hungary.

Robert Eaglestone is Professor of Contemporary Literature and Thought at Royal Holloway, University of London. His publications include *Ethical Criticism* (1997), *Doing English* (1999, 2002), and *The Holocaust and the Postmodern* (2004). He is the series editor of *Routledge Critical Thinkers*.

Rachel Falconer is Reader in English Literature in the School of English at the University of Sheffield, where she teaches contemporary literature and theory. Her current research interests are in katabatic narrative (descents to Hell), magic realism, fantasy, Holocaust literature, children's literature, and narrative theory, and she supervises Ph.D.s in these areas. She has recently published *Hell in Contemporary Literature: Western Descent Narratives since 1945* (2005). She is currently working on a volume called *Crossover Literature and Cross-Reading in the UK* (2007).

Nicola King is Senior Lecturer in English at the University of the West of England. She is the author of *Memory, Narrative, Identity: Remembering the Self* (2000) and articles on popular and contemporary fiction, the writing of the Holocaust, and memory work.

Barry Langford is Senior Lecturer in Film Studies at Royal Holloway, University of London. He is the author of *Film Genre: Hollywood and Beyond* (2005) and essays on a wide variety of subjects in film and media studies and critical theory, including unrepresentability in Holocaust film; Chris Marker's politics; revisionist Westerns; narrative temporalities in *The Lord of the Rings*; images of disaster in Michel de Certeau; American identity in 1970s Hollywood; modernity and trauma in Walter Benjamin and Siegfried Kracauer; exilic identities in European city films; and the political unconscious of TV sitcoms. He has also written two Holocaust-themed screenplays, the short *Torte Bluma* (2005), and the feature film *Seven Blades of Grass* (currently in production).

Antony Rowland is Senior Lecturer in English at the University of Salford. He teaches the Holocaust at both undergraduate and postgraduate levels and supervises research in this area. He has recently published *Holocaust Poetry* (2005) and *Tony Harrison and the Holocaust* (2001). He is currently co-editing volumes on memory, masculinity, and Holocaust poetry, and writing a monograph on testimony.

Libby Saxton is Lecturer in French and Film Studies in the School of Languages, Linguistics, and Film at Queen Mary, University of London. She teaches Holocaust film at both undergraduate and postgraduate levels. She is the author of *Haunted Images: Film, Ethics, Testimony and the Holocaust* (2007), and a series of essays on the interaction between post-war French cinema and thought, and co-editor of *Seeing Things: Vision, Perception and Interpretation in French Studies* (2002). She is currently working on a co-authored book, *Cinema and Ethics: Foreclosed Encounters* (2008–9).

R. Clifton Spargo, a fiction writer and critic, is Associate Professor of English at Marquette University. Formerly the Pearl Resnick Fellow at the Center for Advanced Holocaust Studies of the US Holocaust Memorial Museum, he is the author of *The Ethics of Mourning* (2004), and *Vigilant Memory: Emmanuel Levinas, the Holocaust, and the Unjust Death* (2006), and is co-editor with Robert Ehrenreich of *After Representation?: the Holocaust, Literature, and Culture* (forthcoming 2008).

Ursula Tidd is Senior Lecturer in French Studies at the University of Manchester, UK. Her research interests are the literature and philosophy of Simone de Beauvoir, and post-war French culture and thought, with a current focus on the representation of Holocaust experience in French literature and film. She has published two monographs on Simone de Beauvoir: *Simone de Beauvoir, Gender and Testimony* (1999), and *Simone de Beauvoir*, an introduction to Beauvoir's thought (2004). She has also recently authored articles and chapters on Beauvoir's *Les Mandarins* and *Les belles images*, Sartre's *La Nausée* and the Holocaust testimonies of Jorge Semprún. Her current projects include a critical biography of Simone de Beauvoir.

Sue Vice is Professor of English Literature at the University of Sheffield. Her most recent books are *Holocaust Fiction* (2000), and *Children Writing the Holocaust* (2004). She is currently working on a study of the television dramatist Jack Rosenthal for Manchester University Press.

Anne Whitehead is Senior Lecturer in Contemporary Literature and Theory in the School of English at the University of Newcastle upon Tyne. She teaches the Holocaust at both undergraduate and postgraduate levels and supervises research in this area. She has recently published *Trauma Fiction* (2004) and *W. G. Sebald—A Critical Companion* (2004). She is currently co-editing *Theories of Memory: a Reader* (2007) and is writing a volume on *Memory* for the Routledge New Critical Idioms series.

Introduction
Robert Eaglestone and Barry Langford

The French philosopher Jean-François Lyotard surmised that the shock of the Holocaust was so great that it destroyed the very instruments by which it could have been measured. But the aftershocks *are* measurable: we are deep into the process of creating new instruments to record and express what happened. The instruments themselves, the means of expression are now, as it were, born of trauma.

Geoffrey Hartmann.[1]

The new instruments to which Geoffrey Hartmann points do not only record and express the events of the Holocaust: they also teach it. And it is this teaching, and the particular and significant issues the subject matter raises in teaching, which this volume aims to address.

Not only has the Holocaust—and this is already a contested term—become a major topic of research, but, in the last twenty years or so, teaching the Holocaust has spread from departments of History and Political Science right across the arts, humanities, and socials sciences curriculum. Indeed, in literary studies, modern languages, and film studies, the subjects of interest here, there has been a significant surge in interest: in literary studies, for example, the area has grown from one course nationally in 1996 (Sue Vice's in Sheffield) to nine courses in 2003.[2] Moreover, as there is more research done in the area, these sorts of texts ("born of trauma") have become more widely studied across the literature, film, and media curriculum. In 2005, the English Subject Centre ran a national conference on these issues which attracted over 50 delegates.

The area is, correctly, fraught with difficulties. Many of these circle around "binary oppositions" of do we?/should we?; silence/speech; history/fiction; literary/non-literary; testimony/fiction; perpetrators/victims; isolating Holocaust studies/locating it in the mainstream; affect/rigour; appropriate/inappropriate; scholarship/respect for the dead or memory. Interestingly, many of these in literary pedagogy reflect research or debates in the wider field of Holocaust studies: the tension between scholarship and respect for the dead, for example, has been the focus of a series of acrimonious debates between historians, curators, survivors and their families, and others. But to see these as oppositions is perhaps a mistake: perhaps they mark phases in a dialectics, awaiting research and reflection on Holocaust pedagogy as the area develops and deepens.

Problems of pedagogy

The chapters in this book circle around similar sets of questions and worries: it may be worth highlighting a few of them here. Perhaps one of the most interesting and important, though hardest to pin down, stems from the sense that this subject is seen to be, in some complex and profound way, different from other areas in the curriculum. Its content—mass death, destruction, immense human suffering, a cataclysm— and its continuing impact in many different fora seems, at first perhaps, to set it apart. Whether this is actually the case or not, this phenomena creates expectations in teachers and, more importantly, in students that can in themselves be problematic. One symptom of this is what Gillian Rose called "Holocaust Piety," a mystification "of something we dare not understand."[3] This "piety" causes difficulties and pedagogic problems: for example, it can lead to teachers self-censoring their teaching from a desire not to upset the students, or (conversely) the students not pushing an idea or critical concept fully. It also affects normal pedagogic language: talking about Holocaust survivors as a teaching "resource," normal in pedagogy jargon ("what resources are there?"), has a different and unsettling timbre in this context. On the other hand, this feeling also lies behind the unquestioned high level of student commitment to courses of this sort: students who opted for these courses invest a great deal of time and energy into them. This commitment sometimes leads to issues of identity and identity politics, over a whole gamut of identifications (Jewish, British, Israeli, German, European, American), erupting with great and often disturbing force in the seminar room. It is clear that the "empathic unsettlement" that scholars such as Dominick LaCapra have noted in reading or viewing Holocaust texts is also present in teaching and being taught the subject.

This unsettlement and apartness leads itself to more complex and often unresolved issues. In the first chapter of *Testimony: Crises of Witnessing in Literature, Psychoanalysis, and History*, Shoshana Felman asks an array of questions exploring the relation between "trauma and pedagogy."[4] She goes on to illustrate this with the story of what was clearly a particularly demanding graduate seminar from 1984. The course built up through testimonies by Camus, Dostoevsky, Freud, Mallarmé, and Celan, and then concluded with Holocaust Video testimonies. These, Felman says, provoked a crisis in the class: a silence that then fermented into speech not in the class but afterwards, at the student's homes, in their other classes, with their friends. "They were obsessed . . . They felt alone, suddenly deprived of their bonding to the world and to one another": she argues that the class reacted in this way because they felt "actively addressed not only by the videotape but by the intensity and intimacy of the testimonial encounter throughout the course."[5] Felman describes how she resolved this crisis, by turning herself and them to face their reactions, and to validate the reactions *as* crisis in order to give the reactions meaning. She argues that

> teaching . . . takes place only through a crisis: if it does not hit upon some sense of crisis, if it does not encounter either the vulnerability or the explosiveness of a (explicit or implicit) critical and unpredictable dimension, it has perhaps not truly taught.[6]

Felman's account is particularly dramatic and perhaps her conclusion addresses only the more extreme cases. However, most of us have occasionally experienced teaching courses that exceed the bracket of "course going well/course going badly" and are something else: rather like holding a tiger by the tail, these courses—like Felman's—are exciting, unpredictable, and frightening, and break the frame of "normal" teaching. These sorts of reaction are not unique to Holocaust teaching: for example, there are similar accounts in discussions of pedagogy in relation to women's writing (and my, Robert

Eaglestone's, rare experiences of this sort of experience have occurred in both contemporary philosophy and contemporary fiction courses). However, it is clear that this sort of unsettlement does often happen in teaching the Holocaust. Felman's account shows one way of resolving these issues—by confronting them directly. There might also be other ways to achieve this: use of journals and student personal writing might also help work through these issues. Reading groups, set up informally with academic support, might also form a useful bond to deal with these issues. There are also more informal means of support (friends and so on) as well as more formal support offered by most Higher Education Institutions. Overall, there should be a sense that this is a delicate and complex area, where the pedagogic and affective are inextricably intertwined. In this context, fortunately, it would be a mistake to think these are just issues for students: academics who deal in this area still find themselves upset from time to time. They have often, in their own learning, gone through a version of the same affective process and—in relation to the Holocaust—continue to do so, as further reading or rereading constantly reveals horrors. This may make them more able to think through the issues affecting the student cohort.

These issues, too, ask questions of the nature of pedagogic authority. Felman spells out clearly that, on advice from Dori Laub, a psychoanalyst, she took control of her seminar back and actively led it. In this area, where affective and identificatory response seems to be so powerful, the normal pedagogic authority (which comes from positioning as both "teacher" and "expert") is put into question. That is to say, where often a student speaks from a position of learning, to peers and experts, in this field students can rightly feel that they speak from a position of both identification ("as a German, I feel . . .") and from affect ("I was so upset by this that . . ."). Here, both these positions seem to question the more conventional power relations of a course. And of course these reactions, and the implicit challenge, are right and help provoke the sense of crisis that Felman discusses. However, they are not the whole story. Indeed, there is a moment in many Holocaust seminars where, having recognized the affective impact, there must be a more analytical response and engagement with the issues in question. This is clear, as a simple example, in the move from being upset by a Holocaust testimony to thinking about the role of style and focalization in it. Indeed, this is one illustration of how a simple gesture is related to much in other and wider Holocaust debates. For example, Holocaust museums are both memorials and education centres: sometimes these functions go well together, and sometimes they do not. In the latter cases, museums have to make complex choices. On a microscale, these choices are made by educators all the time, in every pedagogic encounter: here, whether to push the analysis and learning further or whether to stop in silence. The pedagogic authority in this case, unusually perhaps, stems perhaps not so much from superior knowledge nor educational expertise, but having experienced the affective process of engaging with these awful texts, and, rather than being swamped (or, perhaps more truly, having been swamped and having stepped back), engaging and continuing to explore and demand more thought on these texts. Of course, and as suggested above, the educators do also fall back into horrified silence too. There is no real "moving on," but this should not stop analysis: this is part of the meaning of the negativity of Adorno's "Negative Dialectics": a process of dialectic that never resolves into a synthesis, and perhaps this is integral to the field. Coming to terms with this is to realize it as a way of thinking "born of trauma."

Another issue that circles throughout this collection is the question of the relationship between the history of the Holocaust and the texts studied. There is a strong feeling among Holocaust educators in this field that the literary and film texts that came from or reflected on these events are doing something much more than teaching "history" by another means and that these texts stand in their own right as important artistic events, rather than as illustrations to a historical narrative.[7] This would not simply be an question of affectivity, however, and this relationship is of course very problematic.

Teaching Holocaust literature and film and the wider curriculum

There are some aspects of this area which set it at odds with much in the current curriculum and educational climate. Importantly, the field of Holocaust literature is inextricably comparative. By this, we mean that the normal form of UK subject curricula in literary and media studies tends towards the national ("English Literature since 1830"; "The Post-War American Film") and away from the international and comparative. There are, of course, some sound reasons for this: the difficulty of studying texts in translation, for example, and the sheer range of information and context that students might need. However, in this case, and as historians have repeatedly found, the literature and historical record are shaped by precisely the continent-wide—if not worldwide—scope of the event. While there are, certainly, enough texts to teach a course in only one European language, this would obscure, perhaps, precisely the scale and range of the event, and its ramifications. Moreover, the aesthetic and critical responses are also international and inextricable. For example, the work of Primo Levi reappears again and again in different critical and intellectual traditions, and, of course, in novels, poems, plays, and mediations on the Holocaust by other survivors (like Jorge Semprum and Elie Wiesel) and those who were born long after the events (Martin Amis, for example).

More than this, the division between high and popular culture which still informs much in literary studies is often elided by this topic. This may be truer of film studies, where popular films such as *Schindler's List* are studied alongside arthouse releases as well as such challenging and austere modernist texts as *Shoah* and *Night and Fog*. But it is also the case in literary studies, where "high literature" (Geoffrey Hill, Anne Michaels) is taught alongside "bestsellers" (Robert Harris, William Styron) and avant-garde fiction (Georges Perec, David Grossman). Other divisions, too, which often structure the more mainstream curriculum are passed over in this subfield: testimony or life-writing is taught alongside graphic novels (Art Speigelman), fiction, drama, film, documentary, and poetry.

This is not to say that differences are passed over in detail: the different national experiences of those who created texts is crucial. The difference between Levi and Wiesel's work can be explored in part by the contrast between assimilated Levi's return to an Italian national culture and the total murderous annihilation of all Elie Wiesel's cultural touchstones in Hungary. Moreover, American reflections on the Holocaust differ from Western European ones, and these both from the writing of Eastern Europeans: Nobel Laureate and survivor Imre Kertesz, reflecting on Communist Hungary and on the abandonment of the Hungarian revolution by the West in 1956, finds the Nazis, the Russians, the Americans, and the British all on a continuum. However, it is to be noted that intrinsic to this field to date has been a sense that the continental or global reach of the issues has seemed more important that these disciplinary divisions. This may change; one can easily imagine courses on "The Holocaust in American Life," but it seems to us that this wider international dimension is of no little importance. It is also at odds, of course, with much in the British university system.

Canons?

In part as a response to these issues, teachers of the subject in the UK and those at the 2005 English Subject Centre conference expressed great interest, naturally, in the texts that are taught on Holocaust courses. Of course, while there is a difference between a canon (a set of highly valued texts, which work both to form opinions and set research directions, and to put up barriers for admission to a special category), and a curriculum (those texts that can pragmatically be set and studied in a given time), these two concepts do blur, especially as a sub-field is finding its feet. There is not space here to rehearse the debates over canon and canonicity that have played a key role in the development of literary and media studies: suffice to say that it seems that none of the participants in the conference, nor those with whom we the editors have discussed these issues, have been keen to insist upon a canon. Indeed, in this sub-field, where new novels and poems continually emerge, any set canon or curriculum is continually being reworked.

However, across the UK, there has emerged a rough list of indicative texts which are often and successfully taught. In literature, extremely popular—if not universal—were Primo Levi, *If This is a Man*; Elie Wiesel, *Night*; Art Speigelman, *Maus*. Many also teach the following: Primo Levi, *The Drowned and the Saved*; Charlotte Delbo, *Auschwitz and After*; Anne Frank, *Diary*; George Perec, *W*; Paul Celan; Tadeusz Borowski, *This way for the gas, ladies and gentlemen*; Anne Karpf, *The War After*; W. G. Sebald, *Austerlitz*; Robert Harris, *Fatherland*; Anne Michaels, *Fugitive Pieces*.

There are a few teaching these texts: Lisa Appignanesi, *Losing the Dead*; Anita Brookner, *The Latecomers*; Zofia Nalkowska, *Medallions*; Sara Nomberg-Przytyk, *Auschwitz: True Tales*; Cynthia Ozick, 'The Shawl'; Stephan Maechler, *The Wilkomirski Affair*; 'Benjamin Wilkomiriski', *Fragments*; Eva Figes, *Child of War*; Jorge Semprum, *Literature or Life?*;

Ida Fink, *Stories*; Jonathan Safran Foer, *Everything is Illuminated*; Sylvia Plath; Geoffrey Hill; Kindertransport poets.

One thing that was a bit odd about this list is the omission of several well-known novels such as Martin Amis' *Time's Arrow*, and D. M. Thomas's *The White Hotel*. Perhaps their time has passed.

For films, the four most central are (perhaps predictably) *Schindler's List*, *Shoah*, *Night and Fog*, and *Life is Beautiful*. The many others that have been taught include *Sophie's Choice*, *The Pawnbroker*, *Train of Life*, *Jakob the Liar* (in both its GDR and US versions), *The Believer*, *The Grey Zone*, the (in-)famous NBC mini-series *Holocaust*, the BBC documentary on "The Liberation of Belsen," and episodes of the television documentary series *The World at War*, *The Nazis: a Warning From History*, *Auschwitz: the Nazis and the "Final Solution,"* and *People's Century*.

Museums and curating also play a part in pedagogy: the US Holocaust Memorial Museum and Beth Shalom, the new Jewish Museum in Berlin are all considered. There is also a sense that the Imperial War Museum's outstanding Holocaust exhibition is an excellent, if underused, resource for Holocaust literature and film teaching.

Relatively few historians are actually "canonical" or taught on literature courses: Raul Hilberg's *The Destruction of the European Jews* (certainly canonical among Holocaust historians), Christopher Browning's *Ordinary Men*, and Michael Marrus's *The Holocaust in History* are the texts usually cited. Among critics, the leading figures were James Young, Dominick LaCapra, Sue Vice, Shoshona Felman, Cathy Caruth, and Peter Novick, whose cultural history of the "history of the Holocaust," *The Holocaust and Collective Memory*, caused a stir a few years ago. Again, noticeable absences from this list were Lawrence Langer and Des Pres's *The Survivor*, possibly the first book in this field. Again, this shows, perhaps, how much interest there is in this area, and how the field is developing.

Among philosophers and theologians, selections are often used from a range of the following: Hannah Arendt, Theodore Adorno, Emmanuel Levinas, Jacques Derrida, Emil Fackenheim, Zygmunt Bauman, Maurice Blanchot, Paul Ricoeur, and Jean-François Lyotard. *The Holocaust: Theoretical Readings*, a reader edited by Neil Levi and Michael Rothberg, is also widely used.

The content of this volume

In designing this volume, and like the other books in the "New English" series, the editors encouraged contributors, in their reflections on teaching Holocaust literature and film, to speak as directly as possible to their own classroom experiences. It is our hope and belief that the essays collected here, by reflecting in detail on practical issues of course design and delivery (including methods of assessment, seminar organization, etc.) alongside wider conceptual and theoretical frameworks, will provide the most comprehensive resource for teachers in this rapidly expanding field. The appendices, comprising an annotated select bibliography and a timeline of historical events and literary/cinematic responses to the Holocaust, are intended to supplement the nuanced and sometimes profound accounts of teaching the Holocaust gathered here.

Sue Vice and Gwyneth Bodger open the volume with an essay that identifies issues and problems arising from teaching Holocaust literature and film, many of which will be further explored by our other contributors. They introduce two consistent themes of these essays: that teaching Holocaust representation presents unique challenges to both students and tutors, and that learning about the Holocaust can never be simply "learning for learning's sake," but always and necessarily entails an ethical and moral dimension. Indeed, they suggest that the Holocaust challenges dominant assumptions about "knowledge" (not to mention "teaching") itself and how such "learning" is to be conducted—challenges which can make the classroom a charged, sometimes emotional, but also a dynamic and enormously creative space.

Vice and Bodger note, as do several other essays, that compunction about subject matter can sometimes make students unsure about, or even resistant to, tackling the formal aesthetic and ideological properties of Holocaust texts (particularly such unconventional "genres" as testimony) as readily or with the same tools as other films or literary works. As understandable as this might be, it surely makes a powerful case for establishing relevant critical and theoretical parameters as a cornerstone of effective teaching in this area. Robert Eaglestone's essay on the nature and applications of literary and critical theory in teaching Holocaust representation addresses not only the relevance to this field of key cultural theorists ranging from Foucault to Bakhtin but also, and perhaps provocatively, argues for the emergence of a body of work that *de facto* has come to constitute "Holocaust theory." This corpus ranges from overtly programmatic propositions about the Holocaust and its implications for conceptual and analytical thought (including celebrated and/or notorious writings by Theodor Adorno, George Steiner, Emile Fackenheim, and others), to critical historiography and theoretically-informed critical studies whose implications extend well beyond the texts that immediately occasion them.

Anne Whitehead's essay is also specifically focused on questions of "theory": here, how the now-expansive field of memory studies—embracing topics such as collective memory, traumatic memory, and "postmemory"—inform her teaching of both undergraduate and Master's seminars on Holocaust representation. In common with other contributors, Whitehead stresses the ways in which student responses to this challenging and often harrowing material must be carefully handled (not "managed") through pedagogic strategies that open up new critical avenues: at the same time, she importantly warns against projecting onto students the kinds of responses tutors desire (or fear!) they will have.

The gradual crystallization, as discussed above, of a "canon" of Holocaust representations allows us to outline a generic or (Platonic) ideal syllabus: the exemplary course taught and discussed by Nicola King is perhaps as near to such an ideal as any outlined here, including both literature and film, testimony, memoirs, poetry, long- and short-form prose, a graphic novel (*Maus*, of course), and ranging from "high" cultural landmark works by Levi, Wiesel, Lanzmann, etc., to popular fictional works like Robert Harris' *Fatherland*. Like other essays, King's manifests a scrupulous attention to and concern for student experience and articulates a widely shared sense that this subject, perhaps more than others, compels ongoing reassessments on tutors' part of course content and pedagogic strategies.

Canons are of course not limited to older media. Barry Langford's essay reviews the state of play in film and television studies. Once again, the high/low culture dichotomy presents itself as a vexed issue—one as Langford notes frequently played out through the "opposition" of Claude Lanzmann and Steven Spielberg—intensified by Adorno's influential polemics asserting the implication of mass culture generally, and commercially produced and distributed film and television particularly, in the enabling social structures and practices of unfreedom and totalitarianism. Langford asserts the importance of developing classroom strategies and heuristic modes that encourage students to question the critical hierarchies that privilege some forms of cultural representations over others. In pursuit of this agenda, the course he discusses ventures into some challenging and decidedly non-canonical areas—such as "Holocaust pornography" (*The Night Porter*, and the notorious *Ilsa, She-Wolf of the SS*).

Many modules on Holocaust representations possess an interdisciplinary dimension—a large number of the courses discussed in this volume, for example, include films alongside memoirs, novels, essays, short stories, plays, and poems—and similarly some courses (depending as ever on institutional practice) may recruit across disciplinary boundaries. Antony Rowland of Salford University reflects on the experience of teaching such a course to students from programmes as diverse as military history, creative writing, and sociology, amongst others. Perhaps predictably, the writers found themselves entering an institutional minefield as soon as they proposed a course that transgressed fiercely-defended disciplinary—and perhaps more importantly, departmental—boundaries. (These are incidentally problems encountered much more frequently in administratively challenged and cash-strapped UK universities than, for instance, in the USA.) Equally predictably, however, having dealt with these issues it proved to be precisely the variety of students' subject-based knowledge, and the ensuing encounters between those knowledges, that for the writers provided the richest and most rewarding aspects of the course. Differences of (real or perceived) competence in dealing with different kinds of material (testimony and poetry, say) and varying levels of familiarity with non-traditional assessments such as self-reflective statements featured among the fruitful sources of these interdisciplinary encounters. Given the commitment in Holocaust Studies, demonstrated across the range of these essays, to a self-critical and experientially-driven pedagogy, the "Salford Model" may and should prove a source of inspiration for other courses and teachers.

Two essays focus on the especially vexed question of Holocaust memory and representation in post-war France (which seems at the time of writing set to take a new turn with the enormous commercial and critical success of Jonathan Littell's epic Holocaust novel

Les Bienveillantes [*The Kindly Ones*, after Aeschylus]). Interestingly, both writers bring their students to encounter the Holocaust in the context of courses dealing more generally with memory and French culture. Ursula Tidd discusses autobiographical texts by Charlotte Delbo, Georges Perec, and other writers who illustrate the transition in Holocaust literature and testimony from "simple" (of course it never is) testimony to the complex admixture of imaginative and memorial work that characterizes recent and contemporary Holocaust texts. In Tidd's apt phrase, these novels, memoirs, and poems foreground "the problematics of memorial inscription."

Libby Saxton, meanwhile, explores the resonances of the Holocaust in French cinema, a tradition that extends from Resnais' *Night and Fog* to Lanzmann's *Shoah* and beyond to Jean-Luc Godard's millennial video essay *Histoire(s) du cinéma*. Her essay takes as its starting-point Shoshana Felman's troubling and challenging question, "Is there a relation between trauma and pedagogy?" Like many of our contributors, Saxton believes that Holocaust representations "call into question students' and teachers' preexisting conceptual frameworks." Saxton's authoritative grasp of the intricate politics of collective memory in post-war France allows her to guide students through the maze of (continuing) critical debate around these films and examine the relationship of affect and analysis in their own responses to these texts.

While most of the courses discussed are exclusively concerned with Holocaust representation, an important and instructive exception is Rachel Falconer's account of teaching Primo Levi's *If This Is a Man* as the fulcrum of a course examining the tradition of *katabasis*—narratives of descent into the Underworld—in western literature. Falconer shows not only how Levi's writing is itself clearly and strongly influenced by that tradition (as an Italian writer, Levi of course bears a profound debt of influence to Dante), but also how subsequent infernal narratives operate in the shadow of "our Holocaust inheritance." Levi thus provides an example of a preeminent writer about the Holocaust whose influence extends well beyond this field, bringing a diverse range of readers—and students—into contact with this historical and imaginative material.

Two other essays examine the ways in which a single text can be "worked through" with students, exploring its multiple socio-historical contexts and valences. Tim Cole demonstrates that a close reading of the 1961 American novel *The Pawnbroker* and the 1965 film adaptation, alongside the critical responses to each, helps history students develop a nuanced understanding of how what today seems a self-explanatory category—"the Holocaust"—with established parameters of interpretation and analysis has in fact evolved through a complex discursive history. The new understandings that emerge from this process challenge students to situate their work beyond narrowly-drawn disciplinary boundaries—a motif of many essays in this collection.

Offering an American perspective, Clifton Spargo nominates William Styron's *Sophie's Choice* as an example of the pedagogically productive "problem text"—a work (like Shakespeare's "problem plays") which defies ready categorization and resists critical attempts to recuperate for socially or aesthetically harmonious ends. Spargo demonstrates that this complex, sprawling and deeply controversial novel—which to many critics has seemed at once to objectify, to appropriate, and to aestheticize the experience of the Holocaust—compels students to measure their own "as-yet undiscerned yet culturally determined" responses against the multi-layered ideological and affective contradictions of the text itself.

The "New English" series argues that "the English curriculum is now a rich matrix of multiple intellectual traditions and cultural interests": we have suggested in this introduction—and the essays in the volume echo this—that this area of study is a particularly demanding example of this. It makes special demands of its teachers and students, because of its relationship to history and to culture, to a range of European languages and to its content. More than this, it is a field where the very idea of "tradition" itself becomes suspect: after all, much of the content marks the destruction of some traditions by other traditions. The study of the Holocaust takes place in, but exceeds, literary and film studies as usually conceived. The "New English" too is "concerned with addressing exciting new areas that have developed in the curriculum in recent years." The study of the Holocaust in literature and in the moving image is new and growing, but its "excitement" is also open to question. The work is gripping, certainly, but not, perhaps, in a way that is easy to acknowledge or to understand. But whatever its relationship to the palimpsest of literary and film studies, this area is now a developing section of the research environment and curriculum. It also brings together many of the desiderata for the field: it is interdisciplinary, wide-ranging, and encourages student commitment.

Perhaps too, the contribution of teachers and students trained in these forms of textual study, and the aesthetic and theoretical issues they raise, contributes to the contentious discipline of Holocaust Studies, which is too often dominated by a narrow view of the historical. A sense of what cannot be pinned down as a datum, or of the affect of texts, or wider questions about authority, genre, and textual range offer much to our understanding of the Holocaust and the world we inhabit after it.

To return to Shoshona Felman's questions about pedagogy and the Holocaust: in a century of "unthinkable historical catastrophes, is there anything that we have learned or that we should learn about education, that we did not know before?"[8] There is, of course, no one overarching thing, no simple lesson or solution: the essays in this volume, focused on the experiences of teaching the Holocaust in literature and film, aim to share practice and understanding in this complex field, but also to do more. They aim to make small, perhaps faltering steps into this terrain. Once again, as Geoffrey Hartman counters Lyotard's assertion of the impact of the Holocaust as immeasurable, these are the new instruments, born of trauma, that allow us, tentatively, to teach the Holocaust. That they are not certain, that they beg more questions than they resolve, that they eschew grand claims, that they are only feeling their way through unmapped ground (to use Agamben's image) are all characteristics that already show some form of deep sense of response to the events.

Notes

1. Geoffrey Hartmann, *The Longest Shadow* (Basingstoke: Palgrave Macmillan, 2002), p. 1.
2. Halcrow Group Limited with Jane Gawthrope and Philip Martin, survey of the *English Curriculum and Teaching in UK Higher Education: a Report to the Learning and Teaching Support Network* (London: English Subject Centre, 2003).
3. Gillian Rose, *Mourning Becomes the Law* (Cambridge: Cambridge University Press, 1996), p. 43.
4. Shoshona Felman and Dori Laub, *Testimony: Crises of Witnessing in Literature, Psychoanalysis, and History* (London: Routledge, 1992), p. 1.
5. Felman and Laub, *Testimony*, p. 48.
6. Felman and Laub, *Testimony*, p. 53.
7. This is discussed at length in Robert Eaglestone, *The Holocaust and the Postmodern* (Oxford: Oxford University Press, 2004).
8. Felman and Laub, *Testimony*, p. 1.

1
Issues Arising from Teaching Holocaust Film and Literature

Sue Vice and Gwyneth Bodger

Situating the Holocaust in the classroom
Gwyneth Bodger

Teaching Holocaust Studies in an English Department presents more practical and theoretical challenges to both students and tutors than does any other course offered. In most cases, students are introduced not only to a new subject of study—the Holocaust—but also to a new genre—testimony—which requires a new genre-specific learning approach and analytical technique. The pedagogical encounter with the Holocaust inevitably confronts two central questions which both complicate and contribute to the ongoing process of teaching—why do we teach, and how do we teach? The former invites an ethical and moral stance on the importance of teaching and learning about the Holocaust: this usually takes the form of a hope that through the remembrance and study of the past, future genocide and atrocity will be avoided and the promise of "Never Again" will be fulfilled. In this context, the Holocaust is not simply a subject for study—learning for learning's sake—but a remedy for the social ills of prejudice, discrimination, and violence.

Bogdan Michalski suggests that Holocaust education can act "like a vaccine" for students, in that it can "immunize them against evil" (2004: 29). Metaphysical medicine aside, this approach to teaching about the Holocaust, while compelling, is flawed for a number of reasons. Universalizing the Holocaust in this way can be viewed as a betrayal of the understanding of the Holocaust as a unique event, thus hindering rather than aiding as full an understanding of the event as is possible for those who were not there. While the uniqueness of the Holocaust or otherwise remains a question for scholarly debate, the notion that the Holocaust provides an analytical lens through which the mechanisms of all genocides and acts of violent discrimination can be observed and studied is problematic. Indeed, Peter Novick suggests that, far from providing a foundation for learning lessons for the future, teaching the Holocaust in this manner actually leads to the creation of a false hierarchy of suffering, in which the Holocaust becomes a "benchmark of oppression and atrocity," the effect of which is to "trivialise crimes of a lesser magnitude" (2001: 14). Indeed, the frequent occurrence of other such crimes since 1945 suggests that Holocaust education has failed, perhaps inevitably, to fulfil the promise of "Never Again," thus laying bare the impossibility of the moral and ethical imperative to teach the Holocaust.

While the extremity of the Holocaust might suggest it to be an ideal starting-point for a wider moral education about racism and anti-Semitism, Michael Bernard-Donals and Richard Glejzer suggest that in fact the opposite is true. To teach the Holocaust through a moral lens is retrospectively to apply contemporary moral and ethical perspectives to a past event in which they played no part and offers at best an inaccurate understanding of the Holocaust: "To found a pedagogy of the Holocaust upon morality is to ignore that the Shoah was a fundamentally extralogical event and that events of history resist interpretation or methodological neatness" (2001: 167). This is not to suggest that the Holocaust should never be taught in the context of racism and anti-Semitism, rather that caution should be exercised in creating too simple a representation of the relationship between racial and religious discrimination, the Holocaust, and genocide. Franklin Bialystok argues convincingly that the Holocaust should be studied as "an event of major importance in the history of modern Europe, with significant lessons and connections to other developments in our time, and not primarily because it is a vehicle for introspection about racism and democracy" (1996: 128). The Holocaust is a subject for study in itself, rather than because of the relevance it may hold for contemporary socio-political and moral ideologies.

Related to this is the concern that an ethical approach to teaching the Holocaust places the tutor in the position of moral educator. A tutor cannot—and should not—govern the meanings and messages that students take away from a class. Indeed, to do so could be perceived as a violation of teaching ethics. As Bernard-Donals and Glejzer point out, "we can't force students down any single path. To do so might be the *moral* thing to do. But to force a moral upon a person leads to certainty, and it was certainty—that Jews were subhuman, that the Thousand Year Reich was the culmination of history—and its logic that led to the Final Solution" (2001: 168). While this point may itself be expressed with surprising certainty, its central tenet that teachers should not act as moral guardians, regardless of the subject, is certainly worthy of consideration.

These problems and complications that lie behind the process of teaching the Holocaust have led Bernard-Donals and Glejzer to suggest a rather bleak future for Holocaust education. They argue that in fact the Holocaust compromises the central premise of the educative process, the transmission of knowledge and information, in that despite the volume of historical and testimonial accounts, the "evidence is not sufficient to provide us with a knowledge of the events" (2001: 159). "Academic discourse," they argue, "necessarily works from the position that the teacher has something to teach, that an encounter with knowledge is universal rather than particular. . . . So it seems inevitable to say that the Holocaust marks the end of teaching" (173–4).

While in a theoretical sense the Holocaust may well precipitate the "end of teaching," in a very practical sense the field of Holocaust study is both vibrant and growing. However, the complexities of the reasons why the Holocaust is taught fuel the methodological difficulties within an educational context. Lawrence L. Langer defines the primary challenge facing Holocaust educators as "the unthinkable in its numerous guises clamour[ing] to burst into the safe havens of our sedated minds" (1998: 194). Indeed, it seems that the study of the unthinkable and of trauma can precipitate a secondary trauma, as Shoshana Felman has termed it, into the classroom itself. In Felman's class, this crisis took the form of an initial silence in the class as the students struggled to confront testimonial material for the first time in an academic context. This silence was followed by an outpouring of emotional and intellectual responses both inside and outside the classroom. On receiving the final assessments submitted by the class at the end of the course, Felman came to the conclusion that the group had "worked through and overcome" the crisis (1992: 52), and reasoned that the experience of crisis in the classroom was actually an integral part of the learning experience itself.

The presence of silence in the classroom was certainly an issue that Sue Vice and I were confronted with during the course on Holocaust representation at the University of Sheffield. The course focuses on testimonial, fictional, and filmic representations of the Holocaust, and students often found it very hard to engage with the material presented in the class environment, particularly at the beginning of the course. Class discussion was at times stilted and difficult, an outcome I believe to be due in part to the nature of the material and to the students' initial inability to assimilate their existing skills in literary analysis with texts that dealt explicitly with the experience of trauma. Silence in the classroom when teaching Holocaust studies cannot be simply dismissed as the product of unprepared or uninterested students. Rather, following Felman's conclusions (1992: 47–56), this silence can be understood as a manifestation of crisis in the classroom. The silence actually represents a participation in the silence that is so often encountered in responses to the Holocaust. Bernard-Donals and Glejzer suggest that "we need to teach *that what we are supposed to know we do not know*," in that students should become aware that a lack of knowledge and understanding of the Holocaust is actually part of the process of learning. The site of learning lies not in what is taught, but in "the gulf that surrounds it" (2001: 174).

Tutors, however, need to create an appropriate pedagogical framework in which silence can be recognized as part of the learning process. This inevitably calls for the development of a classroom discourse which acknowledges the presence of silence and absence within a context of academic dialogue and exchange of ideas. Generating class discussion can be difficult, and in response to this I developed a task-based learning strategy for some of our classes which worked very effectively. Roberto Benigni's film *Life is Beautiful* (1997) met with considerable controversy on its release, and it was decided to use this controversy as a means of exploring Holocaust-related issues in class. The students were given the opportunity to view the film a few days before the class in order to allow time for them to reflect individually on the film. In class, the group was divided into two, and each group was designated a particular task, with one group defending the film and the other presenting criticism of the film. Each group was given relevant film reviews to consider and analyse, and was allowed approximately twenty to thirty minutes to read these through and develop a coherent and reasoned argument for their side of the debate. The groups then took it in turns to present their findings, and the seminar culminated in a class-wide discussion of the issues raised.

This approach was very successful as it offered the students a specific focus for their thoughts, which provided a clearly defined entry-point to the discussion. The small-group discussions also encouraged every student to make a contribution and, by orchestrating a debate in this way, the students were able to engage closely with this particular film, and also critically compare it to other filmic representations of the Holocaust such as *Night and Fog* (Alain Resnais 1955) and *Schindler's List* (Steven Spielberg 1993). In the final discussion, questions of factuality and filmic representation were paramount, emphasizing the necessity of providing students with fundamental background facts. For example, the possibility of the prolonged concealment of a small boy in a concentration camp jarred with the knowledge that such an endeavour would have been highly unlikely in reality. Being able to appreciate potential factual inaccuracies in the film provoked discussion about the juxtaposition of history and representational anomalies in *Life is Beautiful*. It also encouraged a closer interrogation of how a non-fictional film such as *Night and Fog* represents history and memory and strives for authenticity through the means of colour film and black-and-white stills.

The role of the witness in the classroom

Many Holocaust studies courses benefit from the presence of a survivor in the classroom who visits in order to tell their story to the group, and the course at the University of Sheffield is no exception. While the visits from survivors are undeniably powerful and valuable, the specific role of the witness is difficult to define or explain. Students on the course Sue Vice and I co-taught expressed to me their feelings that the presence of an eye-witness in the class was an invaluable part of their learning experience. When I asked one student to expand upon this, she was unable to articulate her feelings fully, commenting that it somehow made the Holocaust more "real," but she herself seemed dissatisfied with this explanation. Nevertheless, this was a commonly held view.

Peter Novick suggests that upon entering a classroom and telling their tale, a survivor transcends their individual status as a witness to the Holocaust and becomes "emblematic of Jewish suffering, Jewish memory and Jewish culture" (2001: 273). It is perhaps this understanding of the survivor as a living symbol of suffering and the Holocaust that allows the presence of the witness to authenticate, to "make real" all that the students have learned from textual resources. However, the experience of our students appears to contradict Novick's view. The presence of the survivor in the classroom did not universalize their conceptions of Jewish suffering, but rather *individualized* them. The physical presence of a single witness contributed greatly to the students' understanding of the mass scale of the suffering in the Holocaust, and served to focus their thoughts on the relationship between history, memory, and testimony. It is perhaps these aspects of the survivor's presence that prompted their initial muteness in the face of her testimony. While this silence was soon replaced by a keenness to talk to the survivor about her experiences, the initial silence does pose questions about the role of the survivor in the classroom. Novick notes that "to be overwhelmed is clearly an appropriate response to this kind of vicarious encounter with the catastrophe. Whether it teaches lessons—whatever we mean by that—is another question" (2001: 260). Novick's comment returns us once again to the particular way in which Holocaust pedagogy functions. The fact that a student is overwhelmed and remains silent is part of the learning process. When studying the Holocaust, the proposition that knowledge is defined as *not knowing*, and that understanding is equally defined as *not understanding* is frustrating for students used to accumulating facts and opinions which eventually lead to a mastery of a discipline. It is this that makes the study of the Holocaust, if not necessarily the Holocaust itself, unique.

However, this currently invaluable presence of the survivor in the classroom poses questions for the future of Holocaust education. Sue Vice noted that students seemed eager to shake hands with the survivor, to somehow make a physical link with the events of the Holocaust through touch. Yet as time progresses, this physical presence of the witness will be lost. Can—or should—this link be replaced, perhaps through second generation survivors, or video testimony? Even to talk in terms of "replacement," with its implication that survivors are regarded as educational resources, suggests that the role of the survivor in education is not fully understood. However, it is a question that must be faced and dealt with if the current model of Holocaust pedagogy is to survive. The alternative, of course, is that methodological approaches to Holocaust education must change and develop: an inevitability if the current flourishing of Holocaust studies is to continue.

Literary genre and teaching Holocaust literature
Sue Vice

Since "Representing the Holocaust" is a course focused on literature and film which narrates a historical event, it begins by drawing the boundaries between literary and historical representation. This can be starkly accomplished by showing students a table entitled "The Final Solution in Figures," giving total numbers and percentages of Holocaust victims in the countries of occupied Europe, which appears as an appendix to Lucy Dawidowicz's *The War Against the Jews* (1975: 479). This can be contrasted with an extract from a fictional first-person account, for instance the following description by Tadek of a selection at Auschwitz in the title story to Borowski's *This Way for the Gas*, which deploys all kinds of literary techniques, ranging from satire and black humour to dialogized polyphony:

> The [SS] gentleman is calm, precise. No truck can leave without a signal from him, or a mark in his notebook: *Ordnung muss sein*. The marks swell into thousands, the thousands into whole transports, which afterwards we shall simply call "from Salonica," "from Strasbourg," "from Rotterdam". (1976 [1959]: 39)

In each instance, the notion of "figures" has an entirely different meaning.

Yet, as Gwyneth Bodger has noted, it is also crucial to establish certain historical facts at the outset of the course. For instance, students are often unsure about the difference between various camps—not only in terms of their function, but in terms of the date of a particular text about them. Of course such uncertainty is not limited to students, as Laurence Rees argues in his *Auschwitz: the Nazis and the Final Solution*. He emphasizes how crucial it is to distinguish between concentration camps like Dachau, and extermination camps such as Treblinka, while adding that "the complex history of Auschwitz" adds to the confusion in the minds of many, as it "was to evolve into *both* a concentration camp and a death camp" (Rees 2005: 23). For students of Holocaust literature, the majority of texts that they study are, for obvious reasons, by or about survival and death in Auschwitz. There are references to Belzec and Treblinka in *Shoah*, and to life in ghettoes and in hiding in works by Ida Fink and Art Spiegelman. However, the difference between camps is not just a historical detail, but is crucial to understanding certain texts. Martin Sherman's 1979 play *Bent*, for example, is set first in Berlin, then in Dachau in 1934. Neither its accuracy nor its possibly allegorical meaning can be properly understood if it is seen as a Holocaust play: rather, it is about the fate of gay men in the days of the pre-war Nazi state, and as such is a fitting allegory for identity politics in the post-Stonewall era in 1970s New York. Indeed, including this text on the course is a useful way to follow up introductory discussions about who were the Nazis' victims, why some groups of survivors have produced more testimonies than others, and whether the term "Holocaust" itself refers exclusively to the murder of the Jews, to all the groups targeted by the Nazis on "racial" grounds, or to a wider definition of civilian victims.

Similarly, Tadeusz Borowski's short stories *This Way for the Gas, Ladies and Gentlemen* can appear puzzling at first. According to the order of the course, students read this collection after Elie Wiesel's testimony *Night* and Primo Levi's *If This Is a Man*, and they wonder how it is in the stories that Borowski's fictional alter ego Tadek receives Red Cross parcels in Auschwitz, and is wracked with horror and fury at having to unload people off trains at the Birkenau camp—but is not sent to the gas himself. Knowing the answer can free students to approach the text in a more successful literary way. Tadek's survival is due to Auschwitz's complex function as both labour and extermination camp, the presence there of political prisoners, and the fact that three weeks after Borowski's—and thus Tadek's—arrival in 1943, it was decreed that no more Aryans were to be gassed. With such factual knowledge, it is precisely the *fictional* detail of Borowski's stories which can be better analysed. The striking literary issue that is raised by *This Way for the Gas* is the choice of fiction over testimony by a survivor. Although this poses no methodological problems for students, it is Borowski's apparently documentary style, in contrast with Wiesel's more literary one, which may cause generic confusion.

Yet getting such facts straight can raise other problems in its turn. The course is about Holocaust *representation*; and in their seminar presentations and assessed essays students are supposed to treat what is for them very new and often distressing material in terms not only of its content, but also—and even more importantly—in terms of its form. Obviously a balance between form and content is a hard one for anyone to get right, and even seasoned critics can lapse into morbid piety or excessive abstraction where Holocaust literature is concerned.

There are particular areas of representation where this problem is posed in an acute way, including the representation of gender, poetry, and film. There are many methodological and literary questions surrounding approaches to gender difference in Holocaust texts. Standard literary theory, which our students have studied in the semester before their Holocaust course, may give pointers that are not always straightforwardly helpful. Is Luce Irigaray's mimesis, Hélène Cixous's *écriture féminine*, or Judith Butler's performativity any help here? Is there any other way to approach gender in Holocaust writing? As critics including Zoë Waxman and Rachel Pascal Bos imply, it is in this area—which students find fascinating and challenging— that the opposition between fact and literariness appears especially starkly, and the challenge to students is somehow to reconcile the two elements.

On the one hand, in his introduction to Liana Millu's stories *Smoke over Birkenau*, Primo Levi points out that the crematoria at Birkenau were "inescapably" situated right in the middle of the women's barracks, and this simple geographical fact defined their existence in the camp (Millu 1998: iv). On the other, Charlotte Delbo's writing seems to be a perfect example of Cixous's *écriture féminine* as put forward in Cixous's essay "The Laugh of the Medusa" (1975). *Écriture féminine* is a poetics based on images of the body, maternity, and bisexuality, as well as "anti-authoritarian" linguistic features such as "play, disruption, excess, gaps, grammatical and syntactic subversion, ambiguities; by endlessly shifting register, generic transgressions" (Guild 1992: 75). The following extract from Delbo's *None of Us Will*

Return appears to display the imagery and linguistic features of *"écriture féminine"*:

> Some came . . . from Zagreb, the women their heads covered by scarves . . .
> some from Greece, they took with them black olives and loukoums
> some came from Monte Carlo
> they were in the casino
> they are still wearing tails and stiff shirt fronts mangled from the trip. (Delbo 1995 [1965]: 6)

In this case, the very unease that students may feel on approaching such a text in this way can be turned into the means of analysing it. It is true that this extract, like much of *None of Us Will Return*, demonstrates disruptive formal features, such as fantastic-seeming juxtapositions, lack of punctuation, shifts between tenses and genders, and a blurring of the line between poetry and prose. But the "anti-authoritarianism" is directed at the deathly authority of arrival at the camp at Auschwitz as much as the rules of grammar and genre. The extraordinary appearance of the people described is the result of the Nazis' actions, and not "fluid figurative language and myths" (Guild 1992).

There appears to be an opposition here between viewing literary texts in terms of historical fact, and viewing them in terms of an avant-garde and even liberatory poetic style. Conventional notions of genre do not help, as the factual-seeming *Smoke over Birkenau* was published as fiction, while the fictive *None of Us* is testimony. One way of uniting the extremes of literariness and history is Mikhail Bakhtin's notion of the chronotope. I always find this a very helpful notion in relation to teaching Holocaust texts, for its combination of "spatial and temporal indicators" in particular historical formations (Bakhtin 1981: 84). On the other hand, this might seem an—even offensively—oblique approach to the simple factual matter of the Nazis' attitudes to gender, demonstrating one's own theoretical mastery rather than attention to the topic itself.

In relation to teaching Holocaust poetry, it is as if the relation between content and form is reversed. There is little danger of students reading the poetry of Miklós Radnoti or Geoffrey Hill as transparently historical documents. My example here is Paul Celan's

"Deathfugue", where the overlap of figurative and literal discourse is the poem's very subject. It is no coincidence that contemporaries and critics of Celan continue to debate whether "black milk", which the poem's speaker claims is drunk in the camp, is an example of camp argot or a poetic coinage to suggest tainted sustenance, or even plumes of smoke. As Celan's biographer John Felstiner puts it, "*Schwarze Milch* insists that in Nazi-ridden Europe, reality overtook the surreal" (1995: 33). Although students find Celan's work hard to approach at first, comparing two well-known translations—one by Michael Hamburger (in Schiff 1995), and one by Felstiner (1995: 31–2)—allows them to gain both a better understanding of the poem itself, and an insight into the process of translation which is implicit in much Holocaust literature. Their preference is usually for Felstiner's more self-conscious version. Not only does he gradually introduce—or de-translate—German phrases, Felstiner also uses a meaningful vocabulary which students readily pick up on. For instance, where Hamburger translates Celan's description of the camp commandant as, "he plays with the serpents and daydreams death is a master from Germany," Felstiner has, "he plays with his vipers and daydreams der Tod ist ein Meister aus Deutschland." In Felstiner's version, as students are always aware, the commandant in "Deathfugue" has deathly vipers rather than Hamburger's allegorical and Biblical-sounding serpents, which are further generalized by his phrase, "*the* serpents," where Felstiner has "*his* vipers."

Conclusion

As we have argued throughout, a course on Holocaust representation taught in a department of English Literature only appears to follow a standard university learning. In practice, both pedagogical techniques and the implications of what is learnt are different. Since the course was established over a decade ago, it has been co-taught by two tutors, often a member of staff and a research student. Co-teaching works against any sense of a monolithic approach, and students have said that they found different approaches by tutors to be beneficial in themselves. Equally, students' learning experience takes place on several levels. Although they are primarily analysing literary and filmic texts as in other courses, students have to assimilate new genres such as testimony and "fictions of the real," to quote Claude Lanzmann's description of his 1985 film *Shoah* (1985: 21). They also have to encounter historical and factual material which is not only distressing and crisis-provoking, but which is crucial for any effective literary-critical analysis. Finally, the subject itself inevitably makes both tutors and students question the very process of university education, particularly in its contemporary form where progress, improvement, "exit velocity," and developmental learning outcomes presuppose a version of the very Enlightenment teleology that the Holocaust throws into question.

Works cited

Bakhtin, Mikhail (1981) "Forms of Time and Chronotope in the Novel", in *The Dialogic Imagination*, trans. Caryl Emerson and Michael Holquist (Austin: University of Texas Press).

Bernard-Donals, Michael and Glejzer, Richard (2001) *Between Witness and Testimony: the Holocaust and the Limits of Representation* (Albany: State University of New York Press).

Bialystok, Franklin (1996) "Americanising the Holocaust: Beyond the Limits of the Universal", in Rochelle L. Millen (ed.) *New Perspectives on the Holocaust: A Guide for Teachers and Scholars* (New York: New York University Press).

Borowski, Tadeusz (1976) *This Way for the Gas, Ladies and Gentlemen*, trans. Barbara Vedder (Harmondsworth: Penguin).

Bos, Pascale Rachel (2003) "Women and the Holocaust: Analyzing Gender Difference", in Neil Levi and Michael Rothberg (eds), *The Holocaust: Theoretical Interpretations* (Edinburgh: Edinburgh University Press).

Cixous, Hélène (1976) "The Laugh of the Medusa", *Signs*, 1, 4 (Summer 1976): 875–93.

Dawidowicz, Lucy (1975) *The War Against the Jews 1933–45* (Harmondsworth: Penguin).

Delbo, Charlotte (1995 [1965]) *None of Us Will Return*, in *Auschwitz and After*, trans. Rosette C. Lamont (New Haven and London: Yale University Press).

Felman, Shoshana and Laub, Dori (1992) *Testimony: Crises of Witnessing, Literature and Psychoanalysis* (New York: Routledge).

Felstiner, John (1995) *Paul Celan: Poet, Survivor, Jew* (New Haven and London: Yale University Press).

Guild, Elizabeth (1992) in E. Wright (ed.), *Feminism and Psychoanalysis: a Critical Dictionary* (Oxford: Blackwell).

Langer, Lawrence L. (1998) *Pre-empting the Holocaust* (New Haven: Yale University Press).

Lanzmann, Claude (1985) "Le lieu et la parole", *Cahiers du cinéma*, 374.

Levi, Primo (1995 [1947]) *If This Is a Man*, trans. Stuart Woolf (London: Abacus).

Michalski, Bogdan (2004) in Jolanta Ambrosewicz-Jacobs and Leszek Hondo (eds), "Let's Teach All of It from the Start", in *Why Should We Teach About the Holocaust?*, trans. Michael Jacobs (Cracow: Judaica Foundation Center for Jewish Culture).

Millu, Liana (1998) *Smoke Over Birkenau*, trans. Lynne Sharon Schwartz (Evanston: Northwestern University Press).

Novick, Peter (2001) *The Holocaust and Collective Memory* (London: Bloomsbury).

Rees, Laurence (2005) *Auschwitz: the Nazis and the Final Solution* (London: BBC Books).

Schiff, Hilda (ed.) (1995) *Holocaust Poetry* (London: Fount Paperbacks).

Sherman, Martin (1979) *Bent* (London: Amber Lane Plays).

Waxman, Zoë (2005) "Testimony and Representation", in Dan Stone (ed.) *The Historiography of the Holocaust* (Basingstoke: Palgrave—now Palgrave Macmillan).

Wiesel, Elie (1972 [1958]) *Night*, trans. Stella Rodway (London: Fontana).

2
Holocaust Theory?
Robert Eaglestone

In the introduction to this volume, we cited Geoffrey Hartman on the creation of "new instruments to record and express what happened" in the Holocaust.[1] The question of these "new instruments" leads to the question of "Holocaust theory": that is, the question of the status of our reflections not only on the events and their representations, but on how, why and with what intellectual instruments we undertake those reflections. What, then, is the role of what is generally called "theory" in relation to teaching Holocaust literature?

This question is significant for three reasons. First, because any form of analysis and pedagogy we undertake is always saturated with the implicit and explicit presuppositions that we bring to our reading, writing and teaching: "theory" in its widest sense is only a reflective awareness of this. Second, because "theory" is now understood as part of the literature and film curriculum, and of course, despite the particular questions this field asks, it is not cut off from the main of Literary and Film studies. As these change and develop, so must the teaching of Holocaust literature. Third, and perhaps most interestingly, the question of Holocaust theory, in a narrower sense as a series of debates and approaches about the representation of the Holocaust, is important because there is a body of *de facto* work that we might now name as "Holocaust Theory." This is characterized (and perhaps made canonical in this field) by books like Michael Rothberg and Neil Levi's excellent collection *The Holocaust: Theoretical Readings* (2003) and Berel Lang and Simone Gigliotti's *The Holocaust: a Reader* (2004) and also by a sense that we can and do regularly turn to a series of well-established debates—over representation, over authenticity, for example—and ideas from well-established figures (Theodor Adorno, James Young, Lawrence Langer, Berel Lang, Sue Vice) who engage in these debates. What do we make of this? And how do we teach it?

In this chapter I am going to explore this issue by aiming to clarify the different threads of theory that we bring to our teaching and reading of these texts. As usual in English and film studies, the word "theory" gets in the way and obfuscates what is at issue: there are a series of different strands at work here which I shall attempt to draw out. Each of these different strands seems to me to present different challenges to the teaching of this subject. These strands are not supposed to be strict taxonomies, but rather gestures towards the sorts of ideas that shape how we teach, and our students learn about, Holocaust texts. Each seems to call for a different pedagogic response.

The first strand of "theory" is made up of the presuppositions and knowledge that students bring to the texts they study, the "always already" knowledge that Nicola King analyses in her chapter in this volume. Unlike some parts of the English curriculum, Holocaust studies is an area which motivates students to "opt in." This implies both a sense of their commitment (over and above their commitment to literature in general) and some previous, if perhaps cliché-ridden, knowledge: they already know more about the Holocaust than they do about, say, the politico-religious debates of the mid-sixteenth century which form the context for *Paradise Lost*. However, this commitment and general knowledge often combine to create an unwillingness to critique these Holocaust texts as they would other works of literature. In conversation, Nadia Valman described a seminar group's growing horror and outrage as she proceeded to offer some acute literary critical points about Elie Wiesel's *Night*: many teachers of Holocaust literature have had similar experiences. Yet, it seems to me that it is these hazy but firmly held ideas, on the part of the students that leads to the perhaps rather oppressive and inauthentic silence of Holocaust piety. (This is not to be confused with what we all sometimes feel, a being struck dumb by the horror.) A task for educators in this case is simply to confront and to challenge, and to risk the "horror" of our students and so to harness and develop this commitment, and open up this bleak pedagogical space for discussion.

It seems to me that, following on from this, that there is a growing amount of what might be simply called "Holocaust criticism and theory," a genre familiar from other areas of literature. These are reflections on the representation of events and I suggest that they can be seen as occurring in four broad chronological waves. The first wave would include reviews and reflections, fragmentary and internationally dispersed, on a range of "Holocaust texts"—for example, Blanchot's essays on Antelme, Adorno's literary reflections and George Steiner's *Language and Silence* (1967). In the 1970s, as historical knowledge and collective reflections of the Holocaust grew, and more testimonies were published or translated, a core of books—a second wave—were published which in some ways laid the groundwork for contemporary literary Holocaust Studies. These include Des Pres's outstanding *The Survivor* (1976) and Lawrence Langer's *The Holocaust and the Literary Imagination* (1975). These, and works like them (Daniel Schwarz's 1999 *Imagining the Holocaust*, for example), are principally concerned with taxonomizing these texts, with bringing them to light and establishing sometimes a canon and certainly a literary context. Often these works argue for the historical or literary significance of these texts. These offer a guide to students, a sense of what the field is or might be. And, while they may have developed the intellectual agenda in a previous academic generation they now look rather dated because many more fictional and testimonial texts have been published, and more avenues of historical research have been pursued.[2]

A third wave of critical reflection seems to me to stem from two extremely important books which succeeded this second wave: James Young's *Writing and Rewriting the Holocaust* (1988) and Shoshona Felman and Dori Laub's *Testimony* (1992). These very different and groundbreaking works do have a number of things in common. Two of these characteristics are relevant here. First, both books stem from the 1980s "turn to theory" in literary studies: *Testimony* explicitly, with its commitment both to psychoanalysis and to de Manian deconstruction, and *Writing and Rewriting* . . . implicitly, through its sophisticated take on historicism and ideas about the nature of the rhetorical dimension of all writing. Secondly, both are concerned with the often overlooked but always felt "oddness" of Holocaust and testimony writing. This oddness is at the core of Felman and Laub's work and, despite its considerable sophistication and influence (on Cathy Caruth, for example), accounts for its purposely unsatisfactory nature. They write that texts "that testify do not simply report facts but, in a different way, encounter—and make us encounter—strangeness."[3] For Laub and Felman, the strangeness cannot be domesticated or accounted for except as strangeness, as the "breakage" of form. James Young, too, is concerned with this strangeness, but for him, in contrast, the central question is how this strangeness is domesticated both by the "epistemological climate" in which writers and readers live and by the very nature of representation itself. His aim is carefully to question and take apart these opposing forces: "if modern responses to catastrophe have included the breakdown and repudiation of traditional forms" then, he argues one response is "to recognize that even as we reject the absolute meanings and answers these 'archaic' forms provide, we are still unavoidably beholden to these same forms for both our expression and our understanding of the Holocaust."[4]

These two books, and the texts that followed them, seem to mark an advance in the study and teaching of Holocaust literature: both bringing these texts into the mainstream and engaging with their particular difficulties. There is a fourth wave in which highly informed and theoretically aware critics take what has been learnt from the study of the Holocaust and think through wider issues in postmodern—or post-Holocaust, or postcolonial—culture using these insights: this might include Michael Rothberg's *Traumatic Realism* (2000) and his current work, Amy Hungerford's *The Holocaust of Texts* (2003), and Peter Berger's *After the End* (1999), Anne Whitehead's *Trauma Fiction* (2004), and Rachel Falconer's *Hell in Contemporary Literature* (2005). These critics—who have parallels in historical writing, too—are less focused on the Holocaust *per se*, but still take it as a central point for their thought. These too, it seems to me, are texts our students should read and engage with. More than this, in the huge surge of interest in trauma, there have been very many books published either explicitly on trauma or that draw on these ideas. Almost all of these have chapters on, or refer often to, the Holocaust and the problems it raises. In the former category are, for example, Kirby Farrell, *Post-traumatic Culture* (1998), E. Ann Kaplan, *Trauma Culture* (2005), and Kalí Tal, *Worlds of Hurt* (1996): in the latter Mariana Torgovnick's *The War Complex* (2005), and Paul Gilroy's *Between Camps* (2000).

And this leads to a third form of theory in teaching Holocaust literature: the ways in which the subject matter itself changes or questions the use of theory. As I have argued elsewhere, many of the sources of contemporary literary theories are themselves responses to the Holocaust.[5] It seems to me that, as has been widely recognized, these Holocaust texts offer challenges to how literary theories are often used. One example here is how Sue Vice in her recent *Children Writing the Holocaust* applies and, more significantly, nuances Bakhtin's idea of "polyphony."[6] Analysing three works—Clara Asscher-Pinkhof's *Star Children*, Henryk Grynberg's *Children of Zion* and Karen Gershon's *We Came as Children*—Vice argues for what she names "choral narration," in which different voices together tell the same overall story. Another example of this concerns debates over intentionality. In the mainstream of literary studies, intentionality has been a subject of debate since (at least) Wimsatt and Beardsley's essay "The intentional fallacy" in 1946, a debate fuelled by Roland Barthes's essay "The Death of the Author." In the study and teaching of Holocaust literature, this debate raises different questions. On the one hand, testimony texts do stand independently from their authors and reveal all sorts of things the authors could not have known, or known explicitly. On the other hand, in this field, it feels absolutely valid to ask about the relation between a testimony text's author and the text, and to ask who it is who uses the lives of the dead. Thus, as Foucault observed, the "'author-function' is not universal or constant," and in this field, as opposed to in others, it has taken on a particular significance to do with the right to speak or write.[7] Thus, in teaching this genre of writing, I think we need to be aware that it is different, and makes different demands of theoretical approaches. This is absolutely not to say that we can retreat from or ignore theoretical demands or questions: indeed, it is to push these demands further, and try to find out how these ideas change around the texts we teach. More than this, as the brief bibliographical survey above suggests, issues that have arisen in Holocaust studies—over trauma, for example—have now become mainstream critical and theoretical topics. Here, oddly, the previously marginalized discourse of Holocaust studies turns out to have a great deal to contribute.

Moving away from Literary studies *per se*, and into the interdisciplinary area that Holocaust Studies inhabits, the fourth sort of theory with which we have to engage is historiography: this is, the occasionally explicit but usually implicit ideas in the work by historians. History is a powerful discourse, especially for the majority of our students, because of the cultural weight and respect given to the work of historians. Indeed, accounts by historians can often sweep over our students with an authority that seems final and limits their responses and interpretations. In part this is to do with disciplinary expectations: literature and film students experience writing about the past in the genre of academic history differently from history students, who are more used to historical controversy and the necessarily contingent nature of historical argument, and so less prone to taking it as authoritative. However, the role of history and historiographical theory is far from clear cut.

First, while the discipline of history has a justified reputation as intellectually conservative, in this field this characterization is incorrect. Not only have the wider historiographical arguments in the last 30 years often taken Holocaust as a "test case" (rather distastefully) but also the Holocaust itself has been the origin of much demanding historiographical thought. The work of Saul Friedlander and Dominck LaCapra, for example, is well anthologized in the "theory" readers I mentioned above. Second, while of course, students of Holocaust literature and film need to know historical data, this is not the be-all and end-all. Contra Berel Lang, I would suggest that history is not the master-genre of Holocaust representation because, indeed, there is no one "master" genre, rather, there are different series of responses to different questions and expectations.

I suggest that the works of history might be explored in three ways in literary and film studies. First, it is important to bring to the students attention the ways in which historians and others have shaped and changed ideas about Holocaust since 1945: the case studies in Tim Cole's *Images of the Holocaust* (1999) are good examples here. This shows how history too, has a history. But it is also important to bring to the fore the unquestioned ideas and blindnesses in historical work. For example, Browning's *Ordinary Men* is one of the most accessible recent historical texts about the Holocaust and one from which excerpts are regularly made available for literature students (from example, in Langer's *Art from the Ashes* anthology). This book presupposes a single, ahistorical human subject. Following the Milgram experiments on obedience to authority—wonderful as a metaphor or pieces of contemporary drama, poor as science— Browning hypothesizes that any human actor from any time could— through peer-pressure and propaganda—become a perpetrator. This "common sense" idea of the time-free sovereign human subject is one that has been called into question by a range of thinkers (Marx, Freud, Nietzsche, Foucault). This is not to say that Browning is wrong in his assumptions, but that his history—like all history—is loaded with extra-historical commitments. Finally, it seems important to me that—*pace* Hayden White—the narrative and linguistic dimensions of any historical writing are foregrounded: this is not (as it was not in Hayden White's case, either) to question the veridical claims made by historians, but to show how they are always shaped and mediated by language. Raul Hilberg is a case in point. Despite his claims to be doing objective positivist history, he also stresses how, in his magnum opus, "one must be a consummate artist, for such a recreation is an act of creation in and of itself. I already knew this fact on the day I embarked on my task."[8] Indeed, his tropes shape his history. His work, in addition to the painstaking reconstruction of the details, is characterized by irony, metonymy, and juxtaposition. The irony ("an irony recognisably suppressed") has often been commented on.[9] The metonymy involves his constant use of parts or the events, individuals, particular examples to express the whole: perhaps this is unavoidable with large-scale histories, but in Hilberg's case it is particularly noticeable. The juxtapositions occurs throughout his work, too: in the first chapter of *The Destruction of the European Jews*, for example, he compares in columns Christian anti-Semitism with the actions of the Nazis. These tropes themselves, especially that of juxtaposition, shape his assertion that the techniques of mass murder "took millennia in the development of Western culture" and so help shape his view of the Holocaust.[10]

The fifth form of texts that our students might look at are more fully philosophical responses, including the work of Adorno and Fackenheim. And in a way, I find this strand of "theory" the most problematic. If we teach, say Fackenheim, are we obliged to teach the roots of his philosophy (in Hegel and German idealism)? When we teach Adorno, do we teach his thought on the Holocaust in relation to the rest of his thought? One of my MA students, with a history background, came to me and complained: she said that she had discovered that Adorno's famous dictum about not writing poetry after Auschwitz was constantly misquoted and misused ("even by historians"). And indeed, it is an idea to which he continually returns, and itself—if it is to be anything other than a banal and actually rather meaningless cliché—is part of his developing thought with a root in his pre-war conversations with Walter Benjamin. Thus, even to come to terms with this, one needs a wider sense of Adorno's philosophy. Now, in mainstream literary studies, even at the more abstract end of theory, it is practically possible (if not really intellectually justified) to draw an arbitrary line between literary reflection and philosophy. However, in the study of Holocaust literature, this seems harder and harder, simply because the texts themselves beg profound historical philosophical questions: what is a person? What is the relation between literature and life? What is an authentic testimony? And so on. It seems to be in a way rather empty not to try, at least, to engage with the more philosophical thought in its own terms, and to offer this to our students.

Conclusion

Of course, this account I have given misses out the most important source of "Holocaust theory": the testimonies themselves. Emmanuel Levinas writes that the cries of the victims of the Holocaust "are inextinguishable: they echo and re-echo across eternity. What we must do is listen to the thought that they contain."[11] And this thought is central. However, just as these texts themselves are constructed from what Young calls the "epistemological climate in which [the writers] existed"—so too are the readings of these texts.[12] Holocaust theory represents the ways in which, in the unavoidable weather of our epistemological climate—a climate in no small way shaped by the events these testimony texts describe—we try to come to terms with the Holocaust.

Do these strands of theory not run the risk of "normalizing" the Holocaust, covering up the events in jargon? In historical discourse, as Saul Friedlander points out, asking normal, historical questions (what happened when and to whom, exactly?) risks "covering over" the horror. One response is to point out that an unreflective or so-called "immediate" response to the events is still shaped by preconceptions and presuppositions, and that "theory" here is about a sense of reflectivity. But more than this, this formalization, this normalization is actually essential to coming to face the Holocaust. This is not because a degree of "detachment" or "callousing" from the affect of horror is necessary (perhaps it is: but it never really comes) but because without these normalizing concerns, there is almost nothing to be said. To "listen" to thought is to be already in a dialogue of sorts, which itself requires speech. And speech requires terms and discussion and so on. For there to be memory, there needs must be the technologies, formal or informal, of memory, the concrete medium through which something is memorialized. In this sense, the discourses of theory that I have outlined make a reflection on this. Indeed, overall, I suggest that these questions illustrate one of the fundamental issues in Holocaust Studies (and, perhaps, in late twentieth/early twenty-first century culture): the irresolvable dialectical process between how our cultural and intellectual discourses shape the Holocaust and how the Holocaust shapes our cultural and intellectual discourses.

Notes

1. Geoffrey Hartmann, *The Longest Shadow* (Basingstoke: Palgrave Macmillan, 2002), p. 1.
2. On recent work in Holocaust history, see Dan Stone (ed.), *The Historiography of the Holocaust* (Basingstoke: Palgrave—now Palgrave Macmillan, 2004) and Dan Michman, *Holocaust Historiography: a Jewish Perspective* (London: Vallentine Mitchell, 2003).
3. Shoshana Felman and Dori Laub, *Testimony: Crises of Witnessing in Literature, Psychoanalysis, and History* (London: Routledge, 1992), p. 7.
4. James Young, *Writing and Rewriting the Holocaust: Narrative and the Consequences of Interpretation* (Bloomington: Indiana University Press, 1988), p. 192.
5. Robert Eaglestone, *The Holocaust and the Postmodern* (Oxford: Oxford University Press, 2004).
6. Sue Vice, *Children Writing the Holocaust* (Basingstoke: Palgrave Macmillan, 2004).
7. Michel Foucault, *Language, Counter-Memory, Practice*, ed. Donald Bouchard and trans. Donald Bouchard and Sherry Simon (New York: Cornell University Press, 1977), p. 125.
8. Raul Hilberg, *The Politics of Memory: the Journey of a Holocaust Historian* (Chicago: Ivan R. Dee, 1996), p. 83.
9. Raul Hilberg, *The Politics of Memory*, p. 88.
10. Raul Hilberg, *The Destruction of the European Jews* (London: Holmes and Meier, 1985), p. 251.
11. Emmanuel Levinas, "Loving the Torah more than God" in Zvi Kolitz, *Yosl Rakover Talks to God*, trans. Carol Brown Janeway (London: Jonathan Cape, 1999), pp. 79–88.
12. James Young, *Writing and Rewriting the Holocaust* (Bloomington: Indiana University Press, 1990), p. 26.

3
The Role of Theories of Memory in Teaching Representations of the Holocaust

Anne Whitehead

In common with other colleagues in English studies, my route to teaching Holocaust representations has been an indirect one. My research interests in theories of trauma and memory inevitably led to an engagement with literature of the Holocaust; as Neil Levi and Michael Rothberg point out in their recent volume *The Holocaust: Theoretical Readings* (2003), "the politics of memory" is one of the main areas in which theory after the Holocaust has been elaborated (3). Questions of memory and representation are inextricable from thinking about the Holocaust, not least because of the often claimed "unthinkability" of the event. My teaching accordingly incorporates a range of theoretical engagements with memory, in order to contextualize and to frame the readings of texts. I draw on ideas of traumatic memory in teaching the literature of the survivors; this material helps to link the suffering of the individual with the broader, collective experience. In teaching the work of the generation(s) after, I turn to Marianne Hirsch's concept of "postmemory," which helps students to understand the ways in which individuals can be haunted by, and define their identities in relation to, events that they have not themselves experienced. I use concepts of collective memory in order to think about the centrality of the Holocaust in contemporary public culture, and to question what investments in the present are served by Holocaust commemorations. In what follows, it is therefore my intention to reflect on the ways in which theoretical approaches to memory have shaped my teaching of the Holocaust, and to suggest the potential value of utilizing these approaches in the classroom.

I currently teach two modules which engage with Holocaust texts. At undergraduate level, I run a module entitled "Representations of the Holocaust." This is open to second- and third-year undergraduates and is taught over twelve weeks by weekly lecture and seminar. The module initially focuses on survivor accounts of the Holocaust, and we look specifically at Primo Levi's *The Drowned and the Saved* (1988) and Charlotte Delbo's *Auschwitz and After* (1995). We then move on to look at the issues raised by visual representations of the Holocaust and the students watch Claude Lanzmann's *Shoah* (1985) and Steven Spielberg's *Schindler's List* (1993). The module closes with texts by the generation after, and in this section of the course we study Art Spiegelman's *Maus I* (1987) and *Maus II* (1992) and W. G. Sebald's *Austerlitz* (2001). The MA module that I run is entitled "Cultural responses to slavery and the Holocaust." This course runs for six weeks and is taught in weekly two-hour seminar sessions. The students focus on a range of representations of slavery and the Holocaust which emerged in America in the 1980s and 1990s. The texts studied include the United States Holocaust Memorial Museum in Washington DC, the representation of slavery in various American museums, Steven Spielberg's *Schindler's List* (1993) and *Amistad* (1998), Toni Morrison's *Beloved* (1987) and Art Spiegelman's *Maus* volumes. In looking at this material, the students are asked to reflect on the political and economic uses to which the past can and has been put.

Teaching the Holocaust to undergraduates

The first section of my undergraduate course is concerned with survivor testimony. As Levi and Rothberg point out, some survivor testimony "engages in precisely the kind of self-reflexive, critical meditation that we call theory" (2003: 25). In this context, I find the writings of Primo Levi and Charlotte Delbo particularly effective in introducing the students to a range of key ideas and concepts. In Primo Levi's *The Drowned and the Saved*, I ask the students to look closely at his discussion of memory, and to think about why he opens his reflections on the Holocaust with a discussion of the (un)reliability of memory. Relating his first chapter to the rest of the work, we then consider the specific act of remembering in which Levi is engaged. We analyse his positioning of himself in relation to the "drowned" of the camps, so that his memory extends beyond the personal to take on the burden of speaking in place of the dead. In negotiating Levi's view of testimony, the students have found it particularly helpful to reflect on the implications of his epigraph from Coleridge's *The Rhyme of the Ancient Mariner*: "Since then, at an uncertain hour, / That agony returns, / And till my ghastly tale is told / This heart within me burns" (Levi 1988: unnumbered).

Like Levi, Delbo also offers the students a complex reflection on memory and what it means to survive. In the lecture on Delbo, I introduce the students to theories of trauma, looking at the "Introductions" from Cathy Caruth's *Trauma: Explorations in Memory* (1995) alongside Delbo's own discussion in *Days and Memory* of "deep memory" and "external memory" (1990: 1–4). I question how one can articulate in narrative a traumatic experience such as imprisonment in Auschwitz, and I suggest that Delbo's "deep memory" provides a useful way to read testimonial writing, including her own. In preparation for the seminar, the students work in groups to analyse selected sections of *Auschwitz and After*, including "Thirst" (1995: 70–5) and "Springtime" (1995: 109–114). The ensuing discussion brings out issues of temporality, fragmentation, subject position, imagery, and the collapse of generic boundaries, so that the students develop their own awareness of the narrative strategies through which trauma is articulated. The seminar examines what "after" means for Delbo, in order to address the ways in which survival is itself a crisis. We also consider the significance of Delbo taking on the voices of other women in her convoy, in the light of Levi's gesture of speaking for the dead.

The next section of the module analyses visual representations of the Holocaust. In the lecture, I introduce to the class the benefits and risks involved in using cinema as a mode of representation. Does film necessarily exploit the memories of survivors by using them as a source for dramatization and financial profit? Does the impetus towards entertainment in film degrade the memory of the victims, or does it reach and touch audiences who might not otherwise engage with this history? What are the limits of cinema, and what cinematic devices could be used to communicate the Holocaust? We look first at Lanzmann's *Shoah*, and consider whether the figure of the survivor on screen acts to make the testimony more effective. The students are asked to contribute to the seminar a discussion of the testimony that they found the most striking, and to justify their choice to the group. We subsequently uncover the levels of mediation in Lanzmann's film, including the staging of scenes (particularly as return or re-enactment), the relationship of interviewer to witness, the role of translation, and Lanzmann's refusal to use archival images. The students are asked to return to their selected testimony (which often involves one or more of these strategies) and to review their decision in the light of the previous discussion. We then move on to look at issues of visual representation in Spielberg's *Schindler's List*. For most of the students, this film represents an important previous encounter with Holocaust representation. We therefore approach the film by comparing the students' memories of watching it initially with their present experience of viewing it in the context of the module. We think about the film as a key representation that has shaped the memory of the Holocaust for this generation. In this context, we discuss issues such as Schindler as hero, the pairing of Schindler and Goeth, the representation of the Jews, and the issues of survival raised by the girl in the red coat or the gas-chamber sequence. I conclude the discussion of visual representation by asking the students to reflect on the contrast between Lanzmann and Spielberg in relation to "high" and "low" culture, in order to complicate their reception of the film and to challenge their assumptions regarding market and audience.

The module closes by engaging with works by the generation after. Here, theories of "postmemory" are used to frame questions of whether the trauma stops with the first generation, or whether it continues on into subsequent lives and histories. We thus return, in a different context, to Delbo's questioning of the possibility and meaning of "after" in relation to Auschwitz. Art Spiegelman's *Maus* gives the students a double perspective that they find highly engaging. They focus initially on Vladek as a survivor who still repeats many of the behaviours and attitudes of the camps. They then extend out to Artie, to consider the ways in which he is caught within a history that is not his own. I have consistently found the students attentive and sophisticated readers of the graphic-novel format, readily able to comment on issues such as page layout, juxtaposition and overlapping of frames, the use of animals and of the mouse mask, and the diminishing size of Artie in response to his emotional state. W. G. Sebald's *Austerlitz* transposes the questions of "postmemory" to the broader context of the generation after in Germany. The students engage with the idea of the "1.5 generation," represented by Austerlitz as a survivor of the *Kindertransport*, and position this in relation to the first- and second-generation accounts that they have studied. We analyse the narrative construction of Austerlitz's traumatic memories, and question the significance of place and architecture in the novel. Particularly effective in this pairing of texts, however, is a consideration of the use of photographs by each of the writers. The students are asked to think of the different contexts of photography—for example, documentary or the family album—and to categorize the photographs in the texts accordingly, indicating their significance in the light of "postmemory." Returning to questions of trauma and narrative, I also ask the students to consider whether the combining of text and images in these works indicates an excessive quality to the narrative; whether there is something here which cannot be articulated in words alone.

In my teaching at undergraduate level, I find theories of traumatic memory useful in framing the textual readings, especially of survivor testimonies. The texts are explicitly concerned with how trauma can be told and heard, and so the theories enable the students to grasp and conceptualize key aspects of the work. Trauma theory also frames discussions of the ethics of identification. Many of the Holocaust texts that we study on the module simultaneously encourage and resist identification, as the reader is involved in the history but also warned that she cannot understand what it was to be there. This is most explicit in Delbo's writing, but arises to a greater or lesser extent in all of the texts on the module. Theories of trauma deal explicitly with the questions of identification that necessarily concern the students when they read Holocaust texts, and Dominick LaCapra's notion of "empathic unsettlement" (2004: 135) seems particularly useful in this context. Related to this, theories of trauma can also be constructive in discussing affect. I encourage the students to be self-aware about how they are positioned in relation to the texts, and to think critically about their affective responses to them. This is not, however, to presume that the students will experience a strong emotional response to the texts studied. There is arguably a tendency in teaching Holocaust literature to project onto the students the kinds of responses that we desire and/or fear that they will have. In teaching representations of the Holocaust, I find as wide and varied a range of student responses to the texts as in any other taught module. Initial reactions to texts range from being moved to tears to being bored to tears, and both of these positions (as well as many in between) can develop into subtle and nuanced critical responses to the material. Theories of "postmemory" provide a conceptual model for a trans-generational space of remembrance, which frames readings of texts by the generation after. More broadly, the notion of "postmemory" encourages the students to consider what it is to be connected to this material. Is the concept limited to familial identification, or does it articulate a more expansive space of identification and connection? If the students are drawn towards a more inclusive interpretation of the term, then can it also be used to frame their own response? If they themselves are the generation(s) after, then what does it mean for them to be touched or affected by this history?

Teaching the Holocaust to postgraduates

My teaching at postgraduate level is more explicitly concerned with theoretical questions. The students are required to engage with a range of theorists on cultural memory, including Maurice Halbwachs, Pierre Nora, James Young, Andreas Huyssen, Peter Novick and Tim Cole. The module also draws on ideas of nation/community and memory, emerging out of thinkers such as Benedict Anderson and Paul Gilroy. In the context of recent representations of slavery and the Holocaust in America, the students are asked to consider how communities remember, and to address the issue of potential conflict between memory communities. The texts that are studied are framed as "sites of memory," and we look at the role and significance of these sites in contemporary cultures. The module broadens out from my undergraduate teaching to consider the relation of the Holocaust to other traumatic histories. Although slavery provides the focus for this discussion, the students often also extend the range of the module to include the history of the Native Americans (this was particularly the case when I taught the module in 2004, which coincided with the opening of the museum of Native American culture on the Mall in Washington DC).

The first two weeks of the module look at the United States Holocaust Memorial Museum, alongside the representation of slavery in various American museums. I divide the class into groups, and give them resource packs which include theoretical extracts, material from museum websites, and museum exhibition guides. I then ask them to discuss key issues such as "location," "design," or "exhibition" and to prepare a presentation for the rest of the group. An identification card used at the Holocaust Memorial Museum has provoked particularly lively debate, leading the students to negotiate issues of identification, and the significance of an emphasis on survival in American commemoration of the Holocaust. We consider the distinction between memorials and museums, and question whether a museum can (and should) serve both functions. We also ask whether a museum serves a different purpose when it is site specific, and think about the circulation and exhibition of historical artefacts given their important role in memory work. I close the discussion of museums by screening footage of the opening of the US Holocaust Memorial Museum, when Elie Wiesel impressed upon President Clinton the urgency of the political situation in Bosnia. In the context of this gesture, we discuss what kind of act is represented by visiting a museum and whether remembering leads to, or potentially substitutes for, political action in the present.

The next two weeks of the module turn to cinematic representations of slavery and the Holocaust, positioning Steven Spielberg's *Schindler's List* alongside his later film *Amistad*. In viewing the two films together, I seek to explore with the students the close connection between them. We watch both of the openings, which create an initial distancing from their subject (the Jews, the Africans) by using a foreign language; this sense of otherness is transformed to sympathy in the course of the film. We then view the extended ghetto-clearance scene in *Schindler's List* alongside the "Middle Passage" sequence from *Amistad*. Both scenes impress on the viewer the indiscriminate violence of the event, and we reflect on the significance of the motif of the Middle Passage in recent representations of slavery, including *Beloved*. The films also share multi-layered endings, which comprise a "plot ending" (Schindler's escape, the conclusion of Cinque's trial); a "historical ending" (information on the post-war histories of the characters in *Schindler's List*, the return of Cinque to Africa); and a "symbolic ending" (the tribute at Schindler's grave, the destruction of the slave fort). Given that the films are similar in so many ways, I then ask the students to account for why they think that *Schindler's*

List was a box-office success and garnered many awards, while *Amistad* did not fare well either commercially or critically. In preparation for this task, I ask them to find and read reviews of both films, so that their response is grounded in the contemporary reception. I conclude the session by framing the films as "sites of memory," both in terms of their own "remembering" of particular histories, and as narratives that—like museums—provide a means by which the (national) community can imagine, represent, and enact its specific relationship to the past.

The module closes by reading Art Spiegelman's *Maus* in conjunction with Toni Morrison's *Beloved*. We look at the ways in which both texts take on an explicitly commemorative function, in acting as memorials (Spiegelman commemorates Richieu, and Morrison all of those who died on the Middle Passage). Both writers are thus concerned to provide a space in which to mourn those who were not buried. The students are asked to discuss, in this context, the issue of how to commemorate absence and the kinds of memorial—or "countermemorial," to use James Young's term (2000: 122)—that would be appropriate to this task. The two texts also share a concern for the trans-generational transmission of trauma, and the relationship between Vladek and Artie is reflected in the bond between Sethe and Denver. We consider the ways in which "postmemory" is inflected by gender in these narratives, as the past is passed on from father to son and from mother to daughter respectively. I conclude the module by asking the students to read closely Morrison's description of "rememory" (1987: 35–6). I then ask them to reflect on the significances of this description for the different texts studied in the course of the module. Students have in past years related the significance of Morrison's spatialization of memory to the theoretical conceptualization of "sites of memory," to the material presence of the museum and/or the cinema as spaces to visit, and to the literary text as providing an alternative memorial space. Morrison also raises the question of whether "nothing ever dies" (1987: 36). This prompts the students to address the issue of forgetting the past, and leads to discussions of whether forgetting is sometimes desirable; whether forgetting is inherently bound to forgiving; and what value there is (for both individuals and communities) in remembering and commemorating past traumatic events.

Theories of cultural memory explicitly inform my teaching of Holocaust representations at postgraduate level. The framework that they provide engages the students with the question of what is at stake for the present in discourses of the past. Their attention is focused on the ways in which the Holocaust has been commodified and the political effects of this commodification. Reflecting on the centrality of the Holocaust in recent and contemporary American public culture inevitably leads to questions regarding the relationship between the Holocaust and other historical traumas. The students are encouraged to use the concepts of Holocaust studies to think about the status of other historical memories, as well as to question whether the assumptions of Holocaust studies are necessarily appropriate to other historical situations. The focus on the politics of memory also raises important questions about the desirability of "victim culture." The students are confronted with questions about the limits of trauma, concerning when and how trauma and identification with the victim are appropriated for political ends.

Conclusion

In this essay, I have argued that texts concerned with the Holocaust are not only important to teach in and of themselves, but they can also provoke stimulating discussions on issues of representation, memory, and the ethics of identification. Many students are drawn to study the Holocaust because of the powerful emotional impact of an earlier encounter, often with a text such as Anne Frank's diary or *Schindler's List*, but sometimes with a visit to the camp-complex at Auschwitz-Birkenau or the Jewish museum in Berlin. The strong reactions that these encounters produce not only motivate students to take the module, but can also help them to think through complex moral and representational issues.

One of the most important questions raised in the classroom has been, for me, that of where we position ourselves in relation to the Holocaust. Discussion of subject position is often the starting point for a textual response in seminars, which leads into the more specific question of identification. In this paper, I have argued that the framework of trauma allows for a self-awareness in relation to issues of position and identification. Too often, trauma in the pedagogical context is problematically equated with, or reduced to, an uncritical identification with the victim. Identification risks being both appropriative and projective; as Dominick LaCapra warns: "it is difficult to see how one may be empathetic without intrusively arrogating to oneself the victim's experience or undergoing (whether consciously or unconsciously) surrogate victimage" (1998: 182). In discussion with students it is therefore important, as Marianne Hirsch and Irene Kacandes point out, "to question the ethics of identification or to explore some of the alternative forms of identification suggested by the works" (2004: 16). I have proposed that "postmemory" can be useful in this context, for it offers a broad space of identification and empathy. Although it emphasizes identification with the victim, this is both modulated and limited by an equal awareness of the distance that separates the participant from the one born after. I have also argued for the importance of exploring with students what it means to encounter the Holocaust from their own, retrospective vantage point. This self-consciousness of looking back from the present will inevitably involve considerations of why the Holocaust occupies so central a place in contemporary public culture and what is involved in the act of remembering. Is student interest in the Holocaust itself, as Hirsch and Kacandes suggest, "displacing the opportunity to consider calamities that have been perpetrated . . . by our governments and fellow citizens elsewhere?" (2004: 19). The question of what is at stake in both remembering and studying this past—the absorption of Holocaust studies into the curricula of higher-education institutions comprises, after all, the formation of an alternative "site of memory"— is therefore as intimately concerned with what is forgotten or disremembered, as with what political and economic interests are served in and through the act of commemoration.

Works Cited

Caruth, Cathy (1995) *Trauma: Explorations in Memory* (Baltimore and London: Johns Hopkins University Press).
Delbo, Charlotte (1990) *Days and Memory*, trans. Rosette Lamont (Vermont: Marlboro Press).
———. (1995) *Auschwitz and After*, trans. Rosette C. Lamont (New Haven and London: Yale University Press).
Hirsch, Marianne and Kacandes, Irene (2004) "Introduction", *Teaching the Representation of the Holocaust*, ed. Marianne Hirsch and Irene Kacandes (New York: MLA), pp. 1–36.

LaCapra, Dominick (1998) *History and Memory after Auschwitz* (Ithaca and London: Cornell University Press).
——. (2004) *History in Transit: Experience, Identity, Critical Theory* (Ithaca and London: Cornell University Press).
Lanzmann, Claude (1985) *Shoah* (Academy Video).
Levi, Neil and Rothberg, Michael (eds) (2003) *The Holocaust: Theoretical Readings* (Edinburgh: Edinburgh University Press).
Levi, Primo (1988) *The Drowned and the Saved*, trans. Raymond Rosenthal (London: Abacus).
Morrison, Toni (1987) *Beloved* (London: Picador).
Sebald, W. G. (2001) *Austerlitz*, trans. Anthea Bell (London: Hamish Hamilton).
Spiegelman, Art (1987) *Maus I: a Survivor's Tale: My Father Bleeds History* (Harmondsworth: Penguin).
——. (1992) *Maus II: a Survivor's Tale: and Here My Troubles Began* (Harmondsworth: Penguin).
Spielberg, Steven (1993) *Schindler's List* (Universal).
——. (1998) *Amistad* (Dreamworks).
Young, James E. (2000) *At Memory's Edge: After-Images of the Holocaust in Contemporary Art and Architecture* (New Haven and London: Yale University Press).

4
Teaching Holocaust Literature: Issues of Representation
Nicola King

At the University of the West of England in Bristol I taught for three years, two of these with my colleague Victoria Stewart, a year-long Level 3 optional module entitled "Representing the Holocaust" within the School of English and Drama. What follows is a reflection on some of the issues that arose during the planning, teaching, and evaluation of this course: I do not claim to have found answers to all of these complex questions, but hope to offer some ways of addressing them with students.

Title and context

The title of the module—deliberately, but more problematically than I realized at first—draws attention to the relationship between the historical event—the Holocaust or Shoah—and the means and processes of representing it. This raises my first and, in some ways, most complex question—is there a way, or should we even look for a way, to give students a sense of what the Holocaust was, "before" or "outside" its representation? Clearly this is impossible—anything we now use as historical "context" is, inevitably, a representation. And yet I cannot help confessing a need to somehow provide students with a bedrock of solid historical fact against which to judge or measure representation itself, in spite of the fact that most students who come to this course do so with some historical knowledge—from school, television documentary, feature film, their own reading—which is already representational. In fact, I sometimes begin by asking them how they first heard or knew about the Holocaust: some cite history lessons, TV documentaries, reading Anne Frank's *Diary* or watching *Schindler's List*—whilst others endorse Terrence des Pres' observation that it is something "always already" known. Students are asked to write a short account of this first encounter or exposure, possibly with reference to their own subject-position as Jew or non-Jew, white, black, or Asian British, male or female, and so on, and to reflect on how these first encounters have shaped their knowledge or understanding, and, later, how these might have changed by the end of the course. I have also shown students the relevant episodes of the BBC series *The World at War* and *The Nazis: a Warning from History*: these documentaries do, of course, raise their own questions about representation and historical interpretation about which students become quickly aware despite their (relative) lack of precise historical knowledge. The more recent BBC history of Auschwitz is useful because it shows how the "Final Solution" progressed in small and often opportunistic stages, qualifying the often totalizing image students may have of the Holocaust.

In these discussions I have told students of my own first encounters and how they affected me: reading Anne Frank's *Diary* in my early teens, being somewhat irritated by her and half-knowing that her story did not end with her last entry; being shown the footage of the liberation of Belsen whilst doing my PGCE, the stunned silence which followed, and the lecturer saying that he felt all prospective teachers should see it; my anger—at about the same time—at Lilian Caviani's film *The Night Porter*, about the sado-machochistic relationship between a Jewish woman and her former Nazi concentration-camp guard. I tell them that these last two experiences led to a long-standing conviction that "art" or entertainment should not be made out of this kind of suffering, and that everyone should be obliged to watch the Belsen documentary and read Primo Levi, and leave it at that. I also tell them how my opinion shifted as my understanding of the complexities of representation in general developed, and how, specifically, reading Perec's part-fictional, part-autobiographical text *W* in the context of my Ph.D. research into the relationship between memory and narrative led me back, as it were, to the Holocaust and an almost compulsive desire to read everything I could find on the subject. There may perhaps have been too much of my own autobiography here, but I wanted students to be honest about their own responses. In raising the question of the ethics or limits of representation, however,

I was not quite prepared for one student's comment—that he saw nothing problematic about using the Holocaust and the images of suffering it involves in art or entertainment—other wars and mass deaths are used in this way, he argued, and he couldn't see why there should be anything special or different about the Holocaust. This was a student who did not stay the course, so I had no opportunity to judge whether or not he modified his opinion. But this exchange foregrounds one of the paradoxes I found at the heart of teaching texts which seek, avoid, or fail to represent this atrocity—of teaching this material whilst also enabling students to understand precisely why so many survivors and cultural commentators and thinkers have acknowledged the impossibility, yet necessity, of representing the Holocaust, or at least its extremes, the mass murder which denied the humanity of its victims.

Syllabus

The syllabus was designed to begin with first-person testimony in the form of memoir, diary, and fictionalized autobiography (a term which acknowledges the highly constructed and novelistic form of Wiesel's *Night*), and then to move on to two very different kinds of film, (one of which includes first-hand testimony of victims, bystanders and perpetrators) to second-generation family memoir, to poetry by survivors and a later American poet, and to various forms of fiction, ending with Spiegelman's graphic auto/biography or "com-mix." This order (roughly) follows the trajectory of increasing distance from the event and privileges first-person survivor testimony—a decision which foregrounds straight away the complex question of the relationship between autobiography and fiction, the assumption that the former might give us a less mediated access to the events or to "history," and the role of fiction in enabling those who "come after" (to use a phrase coined by George Steiner) to become "secondary witnesses" or "witnesses through the imagination" (Norma Rosen). Whilst we wanted to enable students to reflect on these issues and to alert them to the inevitably textual, constructed, and "belated" nature of all autobiography, we nevertheless felt it appropriate to begin with Levi: as Sara Horowitz explains, in the privileging of survivor testimony "[t]he actual experiences of the writer, whether represented or transfigured in the work itself, anchor and validate the writing. The closer the writer to what Primo Levi refers to as 'the bottom'—those murdered by Nazi genocidal practices—the more the work could be construed as itself being a part, a trace, a fragment of the atrocity or at any rate of the survivor's memory or psyche" (1997: 8). I confess to using Levi, at least in part, as this "trace" or "fragment" of actual experience, whilst also drawing attention to the literary and mediated qualities of his memoir, helped considerably by Rachel Falconer's recent analysis of its intertexts and of the important gap or distinction between Levi the naïve new inmate of Auschwitz and Levi the older, more experienced narrator—a distinction it is easy to elide.

The texts are:

Primo Levi, *If This is a Man* (Abacus, 1987) and *The Drowned and the Saved* (Abacus, 1979)
Elie Wiesel, *Night* (Penguin, 1981)
Anne Frank, *Diary of a Young Girl* (Penguin, 1997)
Steven Spielberg (dir.), *Schindler's List* (1993)
Claude Lanzmann (dir.) *Shoah* (1985) (extracts)
Lisa Appignanesi, *Losing the Dead* (Chatto and Windus, 1999)
Aharon Appelfeld, *Badenheim 1939* (Quartet, 1997)
Poems by Paul Celan, Nelly Sachs, Sylvia Plath
Martin Amis, *Time's Arrow* (Jonathan Cape, 1991)
Robert Harris, *Fatherland* (Arrow, 1993)
Bernhard Schlink, *The Reader* (Phoenix, 1997)
Emily Prager, *Eve's Tattoo* (Vintage, 1999)
Art Spiegelman, *The Complete Maus* (Penguin, 2003)

In the first year the course ran, Anne Karpf's *The War After* (Minerva, 1996) was used instead of the Appignanesi as an example of second-generation family memoir, and Anne Michaels' *Fugitive Pieces* (Bloomsbury, 1997) and Georges Perec's *W Or the Memory of Childhood* (Collins Harvill, 1989) took the place of Amis and Spiegelman.

Representation and its difficulties

Questions about representation function on (at least) four inter-related levels: as a question about the role or ability of language itself to represent this kind of atrocity; as a question about who has the right to represent; as a question about literary representation—"the task is to save it from becoming literature," said Cynthia Ozick, and Berel Lang has argued that only the bare chronicle of events is justified; as a question about genre—if "literature" is accepted as a possible or effective mode of representation, what kinds or forms are appropriate?

The paradox here is finding ways to sensitize students to the problems of representation of extreme or traumatic events without making them think that any kind of representation is futile or impossible. This self-reflexive exchange between Art and his psychoanalyst Pavel from Spiegelman's *Maus* puts the paradox in succinct and almost comic terms:

> Pavel: Anyway, the victims who died can never tell their side of the story. So maybe it's better not to have any more stories.
> Art: Uh-huh. Samuel Beckett once said: "Every word is like an unnecessary stain on silence and nothingness."
> Pavel: Yes.
> . . . .
> Art: On the other hand, he said it.
> Pavel: He was right. Maybe you can include it in your book.
>
> (2003: 205)

Students find that Spiegelman's interrogation of his own practice opens up the debate over representation and its limits in an honest and humorous way. For this reason I would now consider beginning, rather than ending, the module with this text, which represents in graphic form the relationship between past and present, memory and history, self and other in telling the intertwined stories of Art and his survivor-father Vladek. I recommend that students read Sara Horowitz's Introduction to her *Voicing the Void: Muteness and Memory in Holocaust Fiction* (1997), which explores the question of representation in memoir and fiction in a very accessible way. At a later stage (or perhaps more suitably at MA level) I give them the more theoretically demanding Introduction from James Young's *Writing and Rewriting the Holocaust: Narrative and the Consequences of Interpretation* (1990) in order to explore more fully questions of interpretation and narrative form. The course circles around five key areas.

(a) First-person testimony

The privileging of first-person testimony in many discussions of the literature of the Holocaust, and in the structure of my course, acknowledges the need and right of survivors to testify—or to keep silent: the question then becomes one of how to read, or how to listen. Langer's analysis of first-person testimony in *Holocaust Testimonies: The Ruins of Memory* (1991) is instructive in exploring how listeners are often keen to impose a narrative of redemption or hope onto the stories they hear, and this can help students become more aware of their own unconscious reading responses. Students are often diffident about "criticizing" first-person testimony, both in the sense of conducting literary analysis and in the sense that they feel they are criticizing the person "behind" the text if they are critical of the text itself. Horowitz comments on how, in discussions of the literature of the Holocaust "questions of morality and 'authenticity' often displace discussions of literary technique and narrative, as though a truly 'genuine' work would read itself" (25). The study of different versions of a text—possible in the cases of Frank and Wiesel—the comments of writers such as Levi and Perec on the relationship between memory and writing, and Caruth's point, as cited by Bernard-Donals and Glezjer, that "testimonial narratives do not disclose history; instead they disclose . . . the effect of events upon the witnesses . . . This realisation leads to the process of examining recent representations of the Holocaust as representations of witness rather than of the event itself" (2003: 13) can all help to enable students to read texts with more analytical confidence. Students may in any case be unfamiliar with reading autobiography and memoir in an academic context: some introduction to theories of autobiography by, for example, Philippe Lejeune and his concept of the "autobiographical pact," James Olney, Paul John Eakin, Susanna Egan, Leigh Gilmore, and Victoria Stewart is useful.

Reading first-person testimony enables students to understand something of the problem of language in terms of the radically different meanings—or connotations—of words such as "cold," "hungry," "oven" and "train" for those who did or did not experience the camps. In more general terms, as Levi put it, "Our language lacks words to express this offence, the demolition of a man" (1987: 32). How can the destruction of a man or woman, as a member of the human race, be expressed in language, one of the defining aspects of our humanity? Robert Antelme writes: "As of those first days . . . we saw that it was impossible to bridge the gap we discovered opening up between the words at our disposal and that experience which . . . was still going forward within our bodies . . . No sooner would we begin to tell our story than we would be choking over it. And then, even to us, what we had to tell would start to seem *unimaginable*" (p. 3), suggesting that the problem of language arose at once, whilst the events were being experienced in the body, not only when he and others attempted to narrate them later, when the problematic processes of memory also come into play, as well as more "literary" decisions about form, register, metaphor, and so on.

(b) The ethics of representation

I take students through Adorno's changing position on the question of representation: we explore what he might have meant, and why, by his comment that it is barbaric to write poetry after Auschwitz and discuss the idea that "The so-called artistic representation of naked bodily pain, of victims felled by rifle-butts, contains, however remote, the potentiality of wringing pleasure from it . . . Even the sound of despair pays its tribute to a hideous affirmation" (in Arato and Gebhardt, 1978: 313). I have found students honest in their response to this, admitting that the representation of violence in film, for example, can afford a kind of pleasure, but also alert to context—one year, many students were also following a course in Gothic Literature and were able to explore the difference between the representation of "fantastic" violence and the representation of the suffering of actual victims. Adorno went on to acknowledge that only in art can this kind of suffering find its consolation: "yet this suffering . . . also demands the continued existence of art while it prohibits it; it is now virtually in art alone that suffering can still find its own voice, consolation, without immediately being betrayed by it" (1962: 312). Texts such as Celan's "Todesfugue" and Michael's *Fugitive Pieces* raise questions about aestheticization and consolation through art: Adorno's suggestion that "Perennial suffering has as much right to expression as a tortured man to scream" (1973: 362) seems to demand a much more raw and unfinished mode of expression.

These questions are developed through concrete examples of the problematics of representation: the scene in *Schindler's List* when we see the women entering what they and we fear might be a gas chamber always provokes intense discussion and some disagreement about Spielberg's decision to film this scene—whether it is "pornographic," voyeuristic, brave in its attempt to represent the central atrocity of the Holocaust or cowardly to ultimately avoid it—I ask students to compare it with the much briefer, and unemotive account of this episode in Kenneally's novel, and to note the more subtle, almost peripheral scenes in the film where we do see prisoners being led to their deaths in the gas chambers. Anne Michaels attempts a very different, "poetic" representation of the gas chambers in *Fugitive Pieces*: she frames this moment with her narrator Jakob's reservations: "I blaspheme by imagining... Forgive this blasphemy, of choosing philosophy over the brutalism of fact" (167–8). The image and the faith it momentarily inspires is quickly admitted to be a "fabrication"—"[e]ven as I fall apart I know I will never again feel this pure belief" (169), but the passage remains. Jakob invokes "[t]he terrifying hope of human cells. The bare autonomic faith of the body" (168) as the dying attempt to reach the last pockets of trapped air:

> At that moment of utmost degradation, in that twisted reef, is the most obscene testament of grace. For can anyone tell with absolute certainty the difference between the sounds of those who are in despair and the sounds of those who want desperately to believe? The moment when our faith in man is forced to change, anatomically—mercilessly—into faith. (168)

This comes some six pages after Jakob's claim that "when the one who can forgive can only speak, there is only silence" (161). A close reading of this passage—reading it side by side with Levi's reflections on the inability of the "drowned," the true witnesses, to speak, Jakob's sometimes contradictory reflections on memory and language, and an exploration of its metaphors—which Michaels develops throughout the text—enables students to explore the paradoxical position of a writer who acknowledges that she cannot speak for the dead whilst also staking a claim for the restorative power of language, and the suggestion, via her geological and biological metaphors, that the deaths of the six million might have had some meaning. It provides a concrete example of the delicate balance between consolation and betrayal through art as Adorno expressed it.

(c) Representation and appropriation

Shoshana Felman bases her theory of post-Holocaust art on the notion that the Holocaust gave rise to a "radical crisis of witnessing" (in Felman and Laub, 1992), disabling the very possibility of testifying in language as well as the writing of history. Here the Holocaust is used as both cause and proof of a postmodern crisis of representation, a problematic position which I try to explore with students. Teaching the literature of the Holocaust does raise the question of whether we, as teachers, might be appropriating it for our own purposes precisely because it does highlight in such acute form the "problem" of representation of extreme traumatic events. A focus on the linguistic and technical features of a text runs the risk, as James Young points out, of ignoring the events themselves: "That is, if Holocaust narrative is nothing but a system of signs merely referring to other signs, then where are the events themselves?" (1990: 3)—a question which many critics have asked of Amis novel *Time's Arrow*, in which the life-story of a Nazi "doctor" is narrated backwards. More dangerously, "As the 'pseudo-revisionists' of the Holocaust have demonstrated by exploiting the ever-palpable dichotomy between words and events, if one can write the Holocaust, and even rewrite the Holocaust, then perhaps one can also *un*write the Holocaust" (1990: 23). This risk was highlighted even more strongly by the discovery that Binjamin Wilkomirski's "memoir," *Fragments* (1995) was, it now seems likely, consciously or unconsciously invented. As Robert Eaglestone and others have pointed out, the genre of testimony has become so well-established that its tropes can be convincingly copied. As Sara Horowitz explains, "One reason that literary texts come to constitute a special category within studies of the Shoah is that, more than other forms of narrative representations, literature foregrounds its own rhetoricity. In fiction and poetry, language is acknowledged and explored not as a transparent medium through which one comes to see reality but as implicated in the reality we see, shaping our limited and fragile knowledge" (1997: 17). This should be a familiar idea to Level 3 or MA students, but Horowitz and others have taken it a stage further in this particular case: "To the extent that literary narrative substitutes language for world, or symbol-making over bare chronology, it uneasily evokes the linguistic mechanisms that facilitated the Final Solution" (1997: 19). We see these "linguistic mechanisms" at work, in different ways, in *Fatherland* and *Time's Arrow*. Postmodern questioning of the ability of language to refer to the "real" in any useful way has its particular dangers here: as Lawrence Langer puts it, "If 'reality' is not accessible in language it will be made more fully accessible through blows. The Nazis themselves, prompted by the sceptical linguisticism of their own time, made the effort to reach beyond words with their ferocious strength" (1991: 41). Levi provides the concrete examples: "here there is no why," he is told by a Nazi guard when he questions the order not to quench his thirst by sucking the icicles hanging outside his barracks window; the prisoners' name for the truncheon used by the guards is "the interpreter." Words, and therefore reality, comes to mean what those in power determine, so that the Jews "become" vermin to be more easily killed, and their murder is concealed by phrases such as "deported to the East." *Fatherland* uses the format of the popular thriller to show how the Nazis' "war on memory" might have succeeded, how the genocide of the Jews might have become "a page of glory in our history which has never to be written and is never to be written" (Himmler, 4 Oct. 1943, Harris 263).

(d) Narrative and representation

Narrative itself raises particular questions about the possibility of representing these events in literary form: Lyotard argued (in *Heidegger and "the jews,"* 1988) that "[n]arrative organisation is constitutive of diachronic time, and the time that it constitutes has the effect of 'neutralizing' an 'initial' violence ... and of staging a recollection that must be a reappropriation of the improper, achronological affect" (p. 16) of traumatic experience: for a fuller discussion of this, see Anne Whitehead's essay in this volume, and the essays of Cathy Caruth (1995, 1996). This is a complex idea, put a little more simply by James Young (although he does not here acknowledge Lyotard):

> It is almost as if violent events—perceived as aberrations or ruptures in the cultural continuum—demand their retelling, their narration, back into traditions and structures they would otherwise defy. For upon entering narrative, violent events necessarily reenter the continuum, are totalised by it, and thus seem to lose their "violent" quality. Inasmuch as violence is "resolved" in narrative, the violent event seems also to lose its particularity—ie., its facthood, once it is written ... For once written, events assume

the mantle of coherence that narrative necessarily imposes on them. (1990: 15–16)

This is a complex idea, but students understand something of the problem when they discuss the closing sequences of *Schindler's List*, when Schindler is transformed into a Christ-like saviour and then breaks down, sobbing that he could have saved more people, and when the mise-en-scène shifts from "his" Jews walking away from the camp, having nowhere to go, to their marching towards Jerusalem to the soundtrack of "Jerusalem the Golden." The denoument of *Eve's Tattoo*, when Eve conveniently breaks her arm just at the point where she had tattooed the number of a concentration camp prisoner, and her lover is able to make love to her for the first time (in her hospital bed) also makes the point, although the ending of this novel is rendered more problematic and interesting by the fact that "Eva," the woman whose number Eve had tattooed on her arm, turns out to have been not a Jewish victim but a Nazi mother.

Lawrence Langer has argued that "*dis*figuration, the conscious and deliberate alienation of the reader's sensibilities from the world of the usual and the familiar, with an accompanying infiltration into the work of the grotesque, the senseless and the unimaginable" (1975: 3) is a more appropriate mode than realism for the representation of the Holocaust, partly because it helps to avoid the possibility of aesthetic pleasure which Adorno warned against. Barbara Foley has also outlined the problems with realism as a literary mode in this case: "the realist novel proposes ethical humanist resolutions that are incommensurate with the totalitarian horror of the text's represented world" (1982: 333), directly contradicting the lack of causality and agency in the world of the camps—"here there is no why." In their different ways, Amis and Harris "disfigure" the world, Amis by narrating his story backwards and Harris by setting his thriller in an alternative past, a 1960s in which Germany won the war, Hitler is still in power, Speer's Berlin has been built and the fate of the Jews is still a secret. Both these novels defamiliarize what has become almost too well known and affect students in unexpected ways: many agreed with me that Amis' evocation of Jewish families being reunited, not separated on the ramp at Auschwitz, and their bodies and communities being reconstituted out of ash and smoke is almost unbearably painful because we know the exact opposite happened. The detective

Xavier March's gradual discovery of the fate of the Jews in Harris' *Fatherland* (although, as Eaglestone points out, this was really the only secret that could have been at the centre of this novel) does, however, re-enact in popular thriller format the coming-to-knowledge of the "always-already" known. One student felt that this novel gave her a sharper sense of how things could easily have been otherwise, and how easy it might be for governments to conceal the truth. It also alerts students to possibiltities, risks, and dangers of using historical documents and facts in fiction, as discussed by Young and Foley. March locates a suitcase which contains the documents—train schedules, map coordinates, orders for materials, an extract from the minutes of the Wannsee Conference, an eye-witness account of a visit to Auschwitz by members of the Nazi government—which provide historical evidence for the "Final Solution": at the end of the text Harris' "Author's Note" tells the reader which of these documents are genuine and which invented, but in the context of Holocaust denial such invention is problematic, and it is interesting that an (invented) eye-witness account from a perpetrator is thought necessary as proof. One of the documents identified as genuine is the report of statements made by Joseph P. Kennedy, the US Ambassador to Great Britain to the effect that "he himself understood the Jewish policy completely . . . very strong anti-Semitic tendencies existed in the US and a large portion of the population had an understanding of the German attitude towards the Jews" (309–10). This alerts students to the fact that anti-Semitism was not a uniquely German phenomenon: Philip Roth's *Plot Against America* (2004), another counterfactual novel in which the anti-Semitic Charles Lindbergh became the US President, would be an interesting comparison here. A novel of a different kind, Appelfeld's *Badenheim 1939* can be taught in ways which bring into question the use of fable or allegory in representation of the Holocaust, and also to compare two very different readings, those of Michael Andre Bernstein, who is critical of the superior position of hindsight implied in the narrative, and Lea Wernick Fridman, who explores the gaps and silences within the text which hint at unspoken and unspeakable knowledge.

(e) Identification

Students and other readers commonly speak of "identifying" (or not) with characters in literature, or, even more loosely, of "relating" to them. This presents another paradox: we may hope that students are moved or even disturbed by survivors' accounts or fictional representations of their experiences whilst also wanting them to be aware of the "illicit and impossible grasping or comprehension of another's real and represented experience as one's own" (Eaglestone 2004: 22–3) in this particular case. This is partly a matter of language, of the meanings acquired by everyday words such as "cold" or "hunger" by those who experienced the camps; it also arises from the lack of shared experience, of a mutually recognizable frame of reference between the world of the camps and the world of the reader, and elements such as causality or human agency which are part of our usual understandings of the world and how we operate within it. Robert Eaglestone has recently explored the process and problems of identification in a range of different Holocaust representations, analysing the tropes and techniques which, in some texts, block or thwart identification. His reading of *Eve's Tattoo* is instructive here, exposing it as a text which attempts to problematize identification whilst also encouraging it. Students readily perceive the ways in which Eve, and behind her Prager, attempt with some desperation to make the Holocaust "relevant," and to show how all women were potential victims of the Nazis. But as Eaglestone points out, identification is a poorly understood process, and one can never predict or prescribe with whom readers might identify. Although I have not done so, it would be instructive to ask students to think of a character from their other reading with whom they have "identified" and to reflect on the process of identification in their chosen instance—did they choose a character close to them in terms of age, gender, ethnicity, or social class, or a character who experienced problems or situations close to their own? Or was their choice influenced by the mode of narrative, and the extent to which it invited them inside a character's head, enabling them to "experience" his or her thoughts and emotions? Were there any techniques or uses of language which made identification more difficult? First-person narration invites identification most obviously, and a diary—apparently the most "immediate" form of testimony—perhaps most temptingly. The case of Anne Frank's *Diary* is helpfully discussed by Susan David Bernstein (in Bernard-Donals and Glezjer, 2003): she explores how close reading of different versions and attention to "Kitty" as the addressee of the diary can shift students from a position of what she calls "promiscuous identification" to "dissonant identification," recognizing the experience of the other *as* other instead of "imagining oneself as the other [which] blurs into assimilating the other into one's own place" (144). Dominick LaCapra makes a similar distinction between "projective identification" and "empathic unsettlement," a difference which can be explored through a reading of W. G. Sebald's *Austerlitz* (2001). Understanding these distinctions is not at all the same thing as experiencing them, although providing students with a more subtle critical vocabulary is important, as is accepting that their responses will vary. When it comes to the representation of perpetrators, Primo Levi takes a hard line on the question of "understanding" and links it to identification:

> "understanding" a proposal or human behaviour means to "contain" it, contain its author, put oneself in his place, identify with him. Now, no normal human being will ever be able to identify with Hitler, Himmler, Goebbels, Eichmann, and endless others. This dismays us, and at the same time gives us a sense of relief, because perhaps it is desirable that their words . . . cannot be comprehensible to us. They are non-human words and deeds, really counter-human, without historic precedents . . . (1979: 395)

This is part of a much larger debate about historical causality, but it is a useful starting point for students interested in the representation of perpetrators, as many are. Amis's *Time's Arrow* and Schlink's *The Reader* offer two examples of how writers of fiction have dealt with the problem of representing characters defined by Levi as "non-human." The reversed narration of *Time's Arrow* and the splitting of the protagonist into Tod Friendly, the former Nazi "doctor" with no memory, and his soul or conscience (following the research of Robert Jay Lifton) both make identification almost impossible, or at least only possible with half of Tod. Schlink's Hanna is a "minor" perpetrator, no Himmler or Goebbels. She is only represented from the outside, through the memories of the narrator, so that her thoughts and motivations remain something of a mystery, although we are offered an "explanation" in terms of her unacknowledged illiteracy.

Conclusion

Student feedback on the module has been almost unvaryingly positive. Several students suggested that the module should remain a permanent, even compulsory part of the degree, whilst others felt that compelling students to take it might prove counter-productive. One student told me later that the module had given her the idea and the confidence to use Wiesel's *Night* during her teaching practice in a comprehensive school; another said that it was the single most important module he had studied. Due to the structure of our degree and the re-organization taking place at that time, I had to decide whether to commit myself to teaching the module every year, or to let it "rest," knowing that I might not get the opportunity to teach it again. Reluctantly, I decided not to continue with it, for a variety of reasons, not the least of which was a fear that my teaching might become stale, that my personal investment in it might diminish. This reason, once again, distinguishes the subject (for me) from other modules where this is less of a concern. I hope to be able to teach it again, and have in the back of my mind an (almost entirely) new syllabus which would raise these issues in different ways.

Works cited

Adorno, Theodor (1962/1978) "Commitment", in Andrew Arato and Eike Gebhardt (eds), *The Essential Frankfurt School Reader* (New York: Urizen Books).
———. (1973) "After Auschwitz", in *Negative Dialectics*, trans. E. B. Ashton (New York: Continuum).
Antelme, Robert (1992) *The Human Race*, trans. Jeffrey Haight and Annie Mahler (Marlboro, VT: Marlboro Press), first published in French as *L'espece humaine* (Editions Gallimard, 1957).
Bernard-Donals, Michael, and Glejzer, Richard (eds) (2003) *Witnessing the Disaster: Essays on Representation and the Holocaust* (University of Wisconsin Press).
Horowitz, Sara (1997) *Voicing the Void: Muteness and Memory in Holocaust Fiction* (State University of New York Press).
Lyotard, J.-F. (1988) *Heidegger and "the jews"*, trans. Andreas Michael and Mark S. Roberts (Minneapolis: University of Minnesota Press), p. 16.
Sebald, W. G. (2001) *Austerlitz*, trans. Anthea Bell (London: Hamish Hamilton).
Wilkomirski, Binjamin (1996) *Fragments: Memories of a Childhood, 1939–1948*, trans. Carol Brown Janeway (London: Picador), first published in 1995 by Judisher Verlag im Suhrkamp Verlag, Frankfurt am Main.

5
Mass Culture/Mass Media/ Mass Death: Teaching Film, Television, and the Holocaust

Barry Langford

In this essay, I will discuss the experience of teaching broadly similar courses on "Film, Television, and the Holocaust" to both undergraduate and postgraduate cohorts.[1] The undergraduate students were single honours Media Arts students whereas the MA students were mostly trained as historians and oriented towards historical study, a divergence of academic experience which produced important and productive differences in how the courses were framed and consumed by tutor and students alike. It would obviously be as futile to try to equip postgraduate history students with a fluency in the often recondite pathways of film theory in a course of ten weeks' duration as it would be, conversely, to try to make undergraduate media students experts in the historiography of the Holocaust. My approach to similar (though not identical) course material with these two distinct cohorts of students has therefore reflected these significant differences.

The course was structured around a series of comparisons and contrasts between material that necessarily often revisits the same or similar historical material, iconography, and tropes (events such as the Warsaw Ghetto uprising, for example, have been recreated several times on film; familiar Holocaust iconography includes the Auschwitz unloading ramp, the *"Arbeit Macht Frei"* gateway, etc; an example of a Holocaust trope is the motif of a spectator looking at the offscreen spectacle of mass death through the peephole of a gas chamber, found in *Holocaust, Amen*, etc.) Purely as a heuristic device,

I suggest to students at the outset of the course that the film and television material on the course[2] may be divided, broadly speaking, into two categories: those texts with an explicit educative or consciousness-raising agenda, or which consciously engage with academic historical interpretation of the Holocaust; and those which exploit and rework Holocaust material in an imaginative, even counter-factual, fashion. The first category is a capacious one that includes both factual and fictive treatments of the Holocaust ranging from television documentaries (*The World at War*, *The Nazis: a Warning From History*, *Auschwitz*, etc.) to dramatic recreations of historical incidents or indeed the entire history of the period (*Holocaust*, *War and Remembrance*, *Uprising*) and works which focus on a controversial area of Holocaust history (*Amen* [the Vatican's alleged complicity with the Holocaust], *The Grey Zone* [the Auschwitz *sonderkommando*], *Conspiracy* [the Wannsee Conference]). In the second category one might find texts with an eccentric generic "angle" on the Holocaust, such as "Holocaust comedies", often marked by a "magical realist" or other non-naturalistic style (*Life Is Beautiful*, *Train of Life*, *Genghis Cohn*, *The Nasty Girl*) or indeed outright exploitation vehicles such as Holocaust pornography (*Ilsa, She-Wolf of the SS*). To which category such celebrated "non-fiction" (as distinct from documentary) films as *Night and Fog* and *Shoah* belong can of course be a topic of fruitful debate.

As the course proceeds, students benefit from being able to compare different dramatic treatments of the same historical material: for example, the recreations of the Warsaw Ghetto Uprising in *Holocaust*, *Uprising*, and *The Pianist*, or the two speculative drama-documentary re-enactments of the Wannsee Conference. The different ideological valences of these accounts (for example, the strongly Zionist emphasis of the depiction of the Warsaw Ghetto Uprising in *Holocaust*), or how these versions, often decades apart, reflect shifts in dominant historical interpretative paradigms, provide rewarding material for class discussion and debate.

Another focus of the course is genre. Considering films in light of their generic orientation helps focus consideration of theoretical propositions regarding the "uniqueness" of the Holocaust: if the Holocaust is unique, does this mandate a corresponding singularity of representational strategies? Where does this leave (the great majority of) mainstream narrative films, which to a greater or lesser degree trade in narrative and representational conventions? Ilan Avisar refers to "the restraints, hesitations, [and] stammers that have become characteristic of authentic artistic response to the Holocaust":[3] but should Holocaust films always be compelled into the modernist strategies this statement invokes (and implicitly endorses) as a benchmark of their "authenticity"? Conversely, considering the ways in which—often hybrid—generic identities are engaged by Holocaust films raises questions concerning the ways in which audience expectations are solicited and manipulated by films: a process which is as true of documentary as of fiction, and of arthouse and auteurist films as of mainstream commercial dramas. While including such challenging works as *Shoah* and *Night and Fog*, by design the course was generally focused on mainstream work in popular cinema and television (with a broad conception of "mainstream" that is not confined to Hollywood or English-language texts). The selection of films also reflected the proliferation of Holocaust-related production from the mid-1990s. These choices together were intended to promote student reflection on the ways in which the Holocaust has been incorporated into contemporary media culture—or even, more tendentiously, is in some degree a "production" of that culture. Such considerations of course carry considerable theoretical baggage; it is with this theoretical material that the course opened, and to which this essay now turns.

Theoretical parameters

"The central task of education today" asserted Theodor Adorno in 1966, "is to prevent Auschwitz happening today."[4] Whether this task is one that education can really undertake—whether indeed the extremity and unique monstrosity of the Holocaust itself makes it ultimately an unsuitable vehicle through which to promote the tolerant, rational, sceptical, democratic, and intellectually rigorous attitudes that would hopefully prevent "another Auschwitz"—of course continues to be debated by scholars and educationalists.[5] What is surely certain is that Adorno would have greeted with incredulity the notion that popular cinema or television could play any part in promoting such attitudes. For Adorno, popular media culture was in an important sense part of the problem, not part of the solution. It would not be overstating the case too wildly to say that in Adorno's view the debased sensibility evident in and propagated through industrially produced mass culture—the "culture industry"—was essentially continuous with the reified instrumentality and technologically-driven irrationalism that in his view characterized both Nazism and the stupefied mass society of "late capitalism."[6]

Adorno's prescription provides a suggestive starting-point for exploring cinematic and televisual treatments of the Holocaust in the university classroom. His powerful (if sometimes crudely generalized) polemics against the culture industry conjoin with his oft-quoted remark concerning the barbarism of lyric poetry "after Auschwitz" to form a forceful position on the problems confronting any attempt to render the Holocaust in the normative terms of popular mass entertainment narratives. Yet these are notwithstanding the forms—*Holocaust, Schindler's List, Life Is Beautiful*—in which the great majority of general audiences have encountered the Holocaust. The great advantage of Adorno's writing on popular culture, despite its tendency towards over-generalization and clear *a priori* judgements, is that his opposition to culture-industry products is not only sociological but aesthetic, and indeed informed by and argued through Adorno's own sophisticated and elaborated aesthetic principles.

Adorno's attitudes towards mass culture offer a sharp rebuke to the unexamined prejudices which students typically bring to the subject—even if their own attitudes often bear the clear imprint, albeit at third- or fourth-hand, of a Frankfurt School-style deprecation of mass culture. Undergraduate students in particular often manifest a somewhat schizophrenic attitude or even a degree of "bad faith" in their attitudes towards popular entertainment in the classroom—perhaps feeling obliged by the academic setting to deprecate and distance themselves from artefacts which in fact they (like all of us) habitually and unselfconsciously consume and enjoy, maybe more than more demanding "high" cultural texts like *Shoah*. Exploring the ways in which Adorno's writings on mass culture are on the one hand a great deal more subtle than they might first appear—for example the auto-critique built into Adorno's writing that recognizes that the deprecation of mass culture comes at the price of social irrelevance (the famous "torn halves of an integral freedom to which however they do not add up"[7])—while at the same time clearly betraying a mandarin elitism, compels students to examine more rigorously the sometimes contradictory attitudes which they bring to their own encounters with popular culture.

Course content

The postgraduate students, who take the "Film, Television, and the Holocaust" module in their second term, thereby come to the course equipped with considerable familiarity with both historical and historiographical issues and—having undertaken modules on philosophical and literary responses to the Holocaust—with aesthetic and theoretical debates too. My introduction to the topic therefore draws on this previous work and seeks to provoke discussion by encouraging students to recognize the continuities between these areas of discussion and the new territory of the course. Beginning with a selection of brief theoretical statements reflecting well-known positions within the debates on Holocaust representation, ranging from George Steiner and Adorno to Gillian Rose, and running the gamut from extreme "anti-representationalist" positions to pragmatic and ethical defences of Holocaust representation, including conventional ones, we proceed to a discussion of three Holocaust documentaries—Resnais' *Night and Fog*, "Genocide", an episode of the landmark 1973 Thames TV documentary series *The World at War*, and finally "The Road to Treblinka" from Laurence Rees' 1999 BBC series *The Nazis: a Warning From History*.[8] Students readily perceive the radically different approaches adopted by each of these films, while also recognizing that the broadcast documentaries both employ operative conventions of mainstream factual programming (conventions which have themselves evolved significantly over the three decades separating the two programmes) that are starkly different from the stylized, modernist mode of Resnais' film. Having already completed modules on Holocaust history and historiography, these students are also able to register the ways in which these films variously reflect shifts in dominant historical paradigms (debates around intentionalism and functionalism, for example, or scholarly recognition of the absolute centrality of racial doctrine to not only the ideology but also the political economy of the Third Reich).

The choice of these three films, widely separated in time, also allows consideration of the ways in which cultural and political context clearly inflects the presentation of historical information. In *Night and Fog*, for example the racial—specifically Jewish—dimension of the Nazi genocide is largely suppressed in favour of a generalized narrative of "deportees'" victimization by "fascists": which may be variously contextualized by the ambivalence about racial categories in the post-war Left, the filmmakers' desire to render (implicit) analogy with the ongoing French colonial war in Algeria, and the widespread incomprehension in the post-war period of the distinctive and unique fate of the Jews amongst Nazism's numberless victims.[9] Discussion of *The World at War* brings out the contradictions involved in an account of the destruction of European Jewry encountered in the context of a large-scale series commemorating a war fought and won well within living memory of a majority of British viewers in 1973, and traditionally freighted with the patriotic sentiment of a "good war." Finally, the commissioning of more recent documentaries within a culture of heightened, even saturated, "Holocaust awareness" raises different questions about the role of popular media as education, commemoration, and as history.

From here the course proceeds to two weeks' discussion of Lanzmann's *Shoah*, which postgraduate students (unlike undergraduates) are expected to view in full. For students with prior experience of examining survivor testimony, Lanzmann's film presents particular problems as its superficial resemblance to testimonial archives (Yale, Spielberg, etc.) masks a fundamentally different—aesthetic—agenda. Amidst the blizzard of published commentary on and discussion of the film, I have always found the transcript of Lanzmann's faculty seminar at Yale in 1990[10] the most useful "way in" to the film, not least as it offers an opportunity to compare Lanzmann's onscreen persona as interviewer/interrogator/interlocutor in the film to the (somewhat lionized) character that emerges from the Yale transcript. Lanzmann's sometimes lapidary, often tendentious and invariably provocative statements about his film and the aesthetic and ethical positions that inform it, and about Holocaust representation in general, offer a rich source of class discussion. Students readily recognize that Lanzmann's claims need neither be taken at face value nor uncritically endorsed, a recognition that can then productively be channelled back into discussion of the film itself, which as Dominic LaCapra notes has in some quarters attracted a reverential reception motivated by a perception of *Shoah* as a metonym of the Shoah itself rather than (as Lanzmann himself has always insisted) a representation.[11]

Approaching the film in this way involves students in a discussion of representational strategies, objectives, and outcomes rather than treating the film as "pure" experience or unmediated testimony. It also helps those students who are perplexed by the film's non-linear organization and tessellated construction (characterized by Linda Williams as "postmodern"[12]) and can easily lead on to a discussion of the manifold ways in which the film "stages" (rather than simply records) history; including, of course, the (in-)famous scene of Abraham Bomba's breakdown in the barber shop, discussion of which typically provokes debate, sometimes heated, amongst students about the ethics of documentary and the degree of conflict between a filmmaker's ideological and aesthetic strategies and the human "material"—here, the Treblinka survivor Abraham Bomba— with which he is working. Given the dimensions of Lanzmann's film, in fact, it may be necessary for the tutor to be more interventionist than would normally be the case, directing student's attention to sequences and passages where the film's many meanings are experienced in a particularly condensed and dynamic way, and which can be screened in class: I have found the aforementioned scene with Abraham Bomba, Raul Hilberg's exegesis of a printed railway timetable detailing a deportation to Treblinka, and perhaps above all the sequence centring on Chelmno survivor Simon Srebnik's meeting with Polish villagers on the steps of the church in Chelmno, to be particularly fertile.

The documentary films seem to pose different questions to undergraduate students and consequently are framed somewhat differently. For these students, in the first place I divide the films into two weeks' viewing, showing the British TV documentaries first before proceeding to *Night and Fog*. My motivations for doing this were twofold: first (and whatever one's reservations about the historical interpretations built into each film), the TV documentaries delivered basic factual information about the Holocaust to students who may have had little or no prior knowledge thereof. Second, as relatively conventionally formatted films, the documentaries allow these media students to discuss formal issues around documentary with which they are familiar (use of voiceover narration, witnesses, archive footage, *mise-en-scène*, music, etc.)—creating if you like a "comfort zone" that students may welcome given the necessarily disturbing nature of much of the course material. This first week thus offers a "launching-pad" for the next two weeks of the course, in which students confront the far more unfamiliar and (albeit in quite different ways) graphic and uncompromising Holocaust representations of *Night and Fog* and *Shoah* (with the first week's discussion divided equally between the two films and the second devoted to *Shoah*). Undergraduates typically manifest a wide variety of responses to *Shoah*—not excluding bafflement and boredom at the film's glacial pace and Lanzmann's apparently pedantic mode of enquiry. It seems important to legitimate (which does not of course mean agree with) such reactions even if they seem unreflective or naïve: after all, as several commentators have noted, the tendency in some quarters to treat *Shoah* as a or even *the* definitive cinematic statement on the Holocaust clearly needs interrogating and this offers as good an opportunity as any.

From here the course in both its postgraduate and undergraduate versions progresses to the best-known and most widely-discussed "popular" representations of the Holocaust, the 1978 NBC mini-series *Holocaust* and Steven Spielberg's *Schindler's List*. The possibly jarring transition from the high seriousness and uncompromising nature of *Shoah* is in fact eased by Lanzmann's own high-profile (and of course dismissive) comments on both series and film, a selection of which are extracted and circulated for group discussion. Discussion of the positions Lanzmann adopts in these texts raises those important broader questions about "high" cultural assumptions about the (aesthetic, political, and ethical) status of mass cultural texts discussed above—and here as noted Adorno can provide a basis for discussion.

Student discussion of popular films can however frequently stall in two areas: first, the uncritical adoption of a dichotomous "*Schindler* vs. *Shoah*" approach to filmic representations of the Holocaust (this is a problem regardless of which "side" in this debate students might take); second, a defence of popular/mass cultural texts grounded in a banally sociological insistence on their greater "reach". Both of these approaches seem to me more profitably framed and critically scrutinized as topics for discussion rather than productive critical strategies in their own right. Undoubtedly the best tool for achieving this is Miriam Hansen's well-known essay on *Schindler's List* and *Shoah*, which identifies and critiques this dichotomous tendency in the reception of Holocaust film and suggests critical approaches to supersede it.[13]

My own preferred strategy is to work with students to uncover some of the cultural and stylistic contexts through which these texts acquire meaning. In the case of *Holocaust*, for example, the blockbuster success during the preceding television season of *Roots*, the epic mini-series portraying African-American experience in the era of slavery, helps account for the network's willingness to invest so heavily in so violent and disturbing a story—another large-scale historical narrative of traumatic ethnic experience.[14] The famously widespread and powerful reactions the series provoked when first broadcast in West Germany, and the critical literature generated by this event, offers another way of broadening discussion out beyond reductive assertions of television's extended (compared to, say, *Shoah*) demographic reach (particularly useful here is Andreas Huyssen's essay on the ways in which the series' success in an avowedly melodramatic/empathetic mode challenged dominant assumptions on the German Left in particular about the superiority of modernist/Brechtian forms of historical representation[15]).

Spielberg's film, meanwhile, relies heavily on subtle, even subliminal generic signals to render its stark subject-matter more amenable to mass audiences. Noticing the ways in which the film echoes—at time even pastiches—such classic Hollywood genre films as *Casablanca* and *Psycho* opens up a rich vein of discussion concerning the virtues and limitations of generic representations of an event which so many writers have insisted remains *sui generis*.[16] This in turn raises the question of "Holocaust film" as a genre, or sub-genre, of popular commercial cinema in its own right, what the generic parameters of this form might be (the foregrounding of survival and/or resistance, for example and the ethical implications of such an emphasis on relatively exceptional events and experiences), and to what extent these can complement or confound historical understandings.[17]

Having tabled issues of genre, the next section of the course dealing with comic, or serio-comic, Holocaust films poses another set of questions around this concept. Clearly for many undergraduate students in particular the notion of encountering so horrific an event as the Holocaust through humour is novel and perhaps unsettling (postgraduate students who have already read Spiegelman's *Maus*, Borowski's *This Way for the Gas, Ladies and Gentlemen*, and perhaps Terence des Pres' celebrated essay on Holocaust laughter, are less taken aback by the concept). The production in the last decade of several films which do employ humour however makes it a compelling and intriguing area for discussion. While Benigni's *Life Is Beautiful* is of course the best known and most widely discussed of these films, I usually find it helpful to screen another "Holocaust comedy"—Elijah Moshinsky's BBC film *Genghis Cohen*, Radu Mihaeleanu's *Train of Life*, or Jan Hrebejk's *Divided We Fall*, for example. These films display a wide range of comic strategies, ranging from surreal farce (*Train of Life*) to comedy of manners (*Divided We Fall*): they also display a variety of ways in which historical fact can be alluded to and commented on, often sidelong. This is important insofar as Benigni's film clearly grossly manipulates and distorts the historical record while at the same time apparently desiring to make an authentic statement about historical experience. Whether such statements are delegitimized by the manifest distortions of history required in order to make them typically provokes energetic discussion of a film that in any case tends to polarize its spectators. Having other texts to hand for comparison and contrast is obviously a useful way to prevent discussion collapsing into a narrow debate between defenders and critics of Benigni's film. (My own strongly negative feelings about the film also make it important for me not to intervene in these debates too partially.)

Questions of the Holocaust's accommodation to and/or appropriation by commercial genre forms were pushed to an extreme in what was undoubtedly one of the most challenging and unpredictable weeks of the course, when I screened the notorious exploitation film *Ilsa, She-Wolf of the SS*. I gave considerable thought to whether or not to include this film on the course, finally deciding having read several scholarly essays on Holocaust pornography[18] which convinced me that this was indeed an important, if distasteful, subject not least for the way in which it necessarily challenged the usually unspoken assumptions about shared liberal values that underpin university teaching (not just teaching about the Holocaust). However, I carefully "framed" this week of the course, explaining to students that the film was indeed "pornographic" (though not in fact sexually explicit), in my view largely devoid of artistic merit, and would certainly be found offensive by many if not most viewers. I stated that students would not be penalized if they preferred not to watch the film (or if they chose to walk out during the screening, as indeed several did). It would of course be possible to explore the minefield of sexualized representations of the Holocaust through a more "legitimate" text— the obvious choice would be Liliana Cavani's *The Night Porter*—but the obvious meretriciousness of *Ilsa* may in fact focus discussion precisely *because* questions about artistic quality, etc., are by and large redundant.

In fact, the class seemed to divide itself almost equally between those who found the film repulsive and offensive (this of course included those who exited the screening) and those who found it merely ridiculous and laughable. In both cases, however, students were very ready to discuss issues around the social tolerance of offensive material; the appeal of exploitative treatments of socially sacrosanct material; and ultimately the more complex question of whether a film like *Ilsa* merely literalizes scopophiliac impulses towards the revelation of the socially unrepresentable with which more ostensibly legitimate Holocaust "entertainments" like *Holocaust* and *Schindler's List* flirt (particularly in their gas chamber sequences). Such concerns provide a provocative frame for discussing Tim Blake Nelson's *The Grey Zone*, a dramatization of the uprising of the Hungarian *Sonderkommando* in the Auschwitz crematoria which courts controversy throughout by self-consciously transgressing the conventionally-observed limits on the graphic representation of the last stages of the "Final Solution" (i.e., the process of extermination in the gas chambers). This film opens up discussion of the attraction to Holocaust filmmakers of the *Sonderkommando*, who figure in Holocaust films out of all proportion to their actual numbers or (arguably) historical significance (as well as *The Grey Zone* they appear in *Holocaust* and *Amen* and of course are awarded a uniquely privileged position amongst the witnesses in *Shoah* by Lanzmann, who regards them as "spokesmen for the dead"). The extreme experiences of the *Sonderkommando* seem to compel attention as examples of "limit experiences", and this can in turn raise questions about the Holocaust generally as a liminal event and the degree to which the ongoing public preoccupation with the Holocaust reflects not only conscience, compunction, commemoration and (literal or metaphorical) restitution but less socially acceptable impulses such as prurience, sensationalism, voyeurism, "atrocity tourism," and the like.

For the last two years I have concluded the course by bringing together the various lines of discussion that have threaded through the term in a context that focuses my own position in an unusual way. I am myself not only an interpreter but a professional creator of Holocaust film texts, as scriptwriter of the award-winning short film *Torte Bluma* (directed by Benjamin Ross). It not only seemed appropriate to include this film on the course—in a "talk the talk/walk the walk" spirit—but it offered an opportunity to compare a Holocaust film that was both by necessity and by intention miniaturist with the tendency to epic scale in many of the most famous Holocaust films. Of course, there was a danger that students would feel inhibited from engaging critically with work by their tutor: this accordingly required me to present the material in as objective a fashion as possible and—by for example stressing the contribution of key creative collaborators to the finished film—stress that the film was in only a very limited sense "mine" and hence was available for critical discussion without compunction. It was of course possible to examine this film in a "privileged" way, not least by comparing both the shooting script and an earlier draft screenplay with the theatrically released film, and to explore the creative choices in making the film as they intersected with the course content. In particular, students recognized that *Torte Bluma* was consciously conceived as in part a rejoinder to the discourse of "unrepresentability" in Holocaust film: while the film itself avoids graphic horror, seeing and representation are explicitly thematized within the text itself, thus relocating questions of what is, or may not be, "seen" away from sometimes abstract questions of the ethics of representation into a key dimension of the interpersonal and affective relations that made the Holocaust possible. The complex—and reciprocal—blindnesses of Treblinka commandant Franz Stangl and *Kapo* Blau enact issues around the relationship to the Other which postgraduate students (who had previously taken a module in Holocaust philosophy) have related in turn to the philosophical positions of Emmanuel Levinas.

Conclusion

As other essays in this volume reflect, many if not most university courses on Holocaust culture and literature include some film material (most often *Night and Fog*, *Shoah*—in part or in full—and/or *Schindler's List*). There are however relatively few courses (in the UK or US) dedicated to the study of the Holocaust and the moving image. It is undoubtedly important to recognize the ways in which Holocaust films enter into dialogue with other relevant discourses, whether as literary adaptations (see for example the respective essays by Tim Cole and Clifton Spargo on *The Pawnbroker* and *Sophie's Choice*), as interlocutors with historical research (cf. Raul Hilberg's explicit modelling of method and interpretation alike in *Shoah*), or simply as cultural productions in the large and fiercely contested discursive field of "the Holocaust" (in which "Holocaust studies" is itself of course very much an actor). In a variety of ways, some of which I have discussed here, this course has aimed to further student understanding of and engagement with these relationships. However, Holocaust films also and increasingly engage intertextually and influentially with one another: for example, Polanski's *The Pianist* may be profitably be read as a response to *Schindler's List*, whilst a comparative analysis clearly illustrates how contemporary critical responses to the latter in large part recapitulate the debates around *Holocaust* over a decade earlier. This is a rich, complex, and evolving chapter of Holocaust representation which demands sustained attention in its own right and not simply as an adjunct to literary study. The primacy of visual culture in contemporary society surely also mandates that students be offered the both the tools with which to interrogate the implications of this visual ascendancy for Holocaust representation, and the opportunity to reflect critically on their own experiences as participants in contemporary media culture.

Notes

1. The course content was broadly similar, although the MA version increased the amount of both viewing and reading required of students: for example, whereas undergraduate students were asked to view the first two hours of *Shoah* followed by a compilation of extracts from later in the film totalling about 90 minutes, the postgraduate students were expected to view the entire film.
2. The course content has obviously varied across the years I have taught this module. In addition to updating the syllabus to include important new productions (*The Grey Zone, Uprising, Amen, Auschwitz,* etc.), at different times the course—reflecting the undergraduate course's rubric, "Media and History", i.e. not simply film and television—has included discussion of Holocaust-related websites (including Holocaust-denial material) and museum exhibitions (the Imperial War Museum's Holocaust permanent exhibit). I will not be discussing these elements of the course in this essay.
3. Ilan Avisar, "Holocaust Movies and the Politics of Collective Memory", in Alvin H. Rosenfeld, ed., *Thinking About the Holocaust: After Half a Century* (Bloomington: Indiana UP, 1997), p. 51.
4. Theodor W. Adorno, "Education After Auschwitz", *Critical Models*, trans. Henry W. Pickford (New York: Columbia UP, 1998), p. 191.

5. See for instance Peter Novick, *The Holocaust and Collective Memory* (London: Bloomsbury, 1999).
6. The *locus classsicus* here is of course the chapter on "The Culture Industry" in Theodor W. Adorno and Max Horkheimer, *Dialectic of Enlightenment*, trans. John Cumming (New York: Continuum, 1973), pp. 120–167.
7. Theodor W. Adorno, "Letter to Walter Benjamin" in Perry Anderson *et al.*, trans., ed., *Aesthetics and Politics* (London: NLB, 1977), p. 36.
8. For 2006–07, this will be replaced by an episode of Rees' subsequent BBC series *Auschwitz: the Nazis and the "Final Solution."*
9. On *Night and Fog*, see Ewout van der Knaap, *Uncovering the Holocaust: the International Reception of Night and Fog* (London: Wallflower, 2006). An excellent account of shifting attitudes towards and understandings of the Holocaust in postwar France can be found in Samuel Moyn, *A Holocaust Controversy: The Treblinka Affair in Postwar France* (New York: Brandeis UP, 2005).
10. "Seminar with Claude Lanzmann," *Yale French Studies* 79 (1991): pp. 82–99.
11. See Dominic LaCapra, "Lanzmann's *Shoah*: 'Here There Is No Why'", *Critical Inquiry* 23 (Winter 1997), pp. 231–69.
12. Linda Williams, "Mirrors Without Memory: Truth, History and the New Documentary," *Film Quarterly* 32 (1991), pp. 357–79.
13. Miriam Hansen, "*Schindler's List* Is Not *Shoah*: the Second Commandment, Popular Modernism, and Public Memory", in Yosefa Loshitsky, ed., *Spielberg's Holocaust: Critical Perspectives on* Schindler's List (Bloomington: Indiana UP, 1997), pp. 77–103.
14. See Jeffrey Shandler, *While America Watches: Televising the Holocaust* (New York: Oxford UP, 1999).
15. Andreas Huyssen, "The Politics of Identification", in *After the Great Divide: Modernism, Mass Culture, Postmodernism* (London: Macmillan, 1986), pp. 94–114.
16. See Barry Langford, "'You Cannot Look at This': Thresholds of Unrepresentability in Holocaust Film", *Journal of Holocaust Education* 8 (1999), pp. 21–38.
17. An important Holocaust film which I have taught on the course, although space prevents my discussing it in detail here, is Roman Polanski's *The Pianist*. As a multi-Oscar-winning, large-scale Hollywood-financed Holocaust drama the film offers many points of instructive comparison to *Schindler's List* (indeed, at one point Polanski's film seems directly to "rewrite" one of Spielberg's more memorable scenes). Students find it particularly interesting that whereas *Schindler* more or less explicitly courted its reception as a "definitive" dramatic statement about the Holocaust— *pace* its problematic emphasis on redemption—*The Pianist* tells a story which is clearly, even defiantly, individualistic and ungeneralizable.
18. See for instance Omer Bartov, *Mirrors of Destruction: War, Genocide, and Modern Identity* (New York: Oxford UP, 2000), pp. 186–218; Kriss Ravetto-Biagoli, *The Unmaking of Fascist Aesthetics*; (on *Ilsa, She-Wolf of the SS*)

Lynn Rapaport, "Holocaust Pornography: Profaning the Sacred in *Ilsa, She-Wolf of the SS*", *Shofar* 22 (2003), 1: pp. 53–79.

Filmography

Amen (Costa-Gavras, Fr/Germ/US 2002)
Auschwitz: the Nazis and the "Final Solution" (Laurence Rees/BBC, GB 2005)
Conspiracy (Frank Pierson, HBO 2001)
Divided We Fall (Jan Hrebejk, Hungary 2001)
Genghis Cohn (Elijah Moshinky/BBC, GB 1992)
The Grey Zone (Tim Blake Nelson, US 2001)
Holocaust (Marvin Chomsky/NBC, US 1978)
Ilsa, She-Wolf of the SS (Don Edmonds, US 1976)
[*La Vita è Bella*] *Life Is Beautiful* (Roberto Benigni, It 1998)
[*Die Schreckliche Madchen*] *The Nasty Girl* (Michael Veerhoeven, Germ 1989)
The Nazis: a Warning From History (Laurence Rees/BBC, GB 1997)
[*Nuit et Brouillard*] *Night and Fog* (Alan Resnais, Fr 1955)
The Pianist (Roman Polanski, US 2002)
Schindler's List (Steven Spielberg, US 1993)
Shoah (Claude Lanzmann, Fr 1985)
Torte Bluma (Benjamin Ross, US 2005)
[*Train de Vie*] *Train of Life* (Radu Miheleanu, France-Romani 1999)
Uprising (Jon Avnet/NBC, US 2001)
The World at War: "Genocide" (Martin Smith/Thames TV, GB 1974)

6
"Representing the Holocaust": an Interdisciplinary Module
Antony Rowland

This chapter will address the issues arising from the construction and implementation of an interdisciplinary Holocaust Studies module at a UK university. As Robert Eaglestone notes in the recent English Subject Centre report on the conference "Teaching Holocaust Literature and Film," there are now many Holocaust Studies modules in literature departments or Schools in UK universities, as opposed to ten years ago (when there was only one).[1] Most of these modules focus, as might be expected, on literature and film: during the conference in 2005, it became clear that the "Representing the Holocaust" module at The University of Salford comprises one of very few co-taught, interdisciplinary Holocaust Studies modules in the UK. It is also the first "cross-School" module in the School of English, Sociology, Politics, and Contemporary History at Salford. Students from numerous programmes (including Military History, Politics, Journalism, English, Creative Writing, Sociology, and Criminology) are invited to take the module in their final semester in level three. The two tutors come from the English and Sociology sections.

Despite the encouragement at a local and national level for interdisciplinary teaching and research, the tutors encountered many obstacles in their attempt to validate the module. These challenges are perhaps indicative of the problems in setting up cross-School or cross-Faculty modules and pathways. Administrative systems are often (perhaps inevitably) tied to subject areas (sections, or departments) at UK universities. Approval for a School-wide module thus encountered some difficulties. One subject area was reluctant to release the tutor into the perceived luxury of an interdisciplinary module based around their research expertise, despite the national clamour for more firmly established links between teaching and research. An innovative, cross-School (and, with the Journalism students, cross-Faculty) module was regarded by some as wasted labour in the sense that the tutors could have been teaching more students from just English or Sociology instead. Other problems arose out of our contention that an interdisciplinary module should make use of forms of assessment coming from each subject area. One subject area did not recognize the validity of project-based assessment, and demanded a definition of a "project," what exactly students were meant to do when engaged in such assessment, and how said assessment was bound up with the learning outcomes for the module. (Thankfully the other subject area already had fully-validated guidelines on projects.) Another perceived sticking point was the tutors' desire to challenge the utilitarian aspects of required "learning outcomes" in relation to the new module. Rather surprisingly for us, the Faculty approvals committee was happy to accept one of the learning outcomes as "the ability to challenge the concept of learning outcomes."

We also felt that the traditional one lecture hour to one seminar hour format did not meet the pedagogical demands of the module. The tutors insisted instead on the creative writing format of a two-hour workshop or seminar. This would allow us to attend to the skill bases and gaps in each subject area, and the troubling aspects of the seminar materials, in a way in which a one-hour seminar would not permit. Journalism students from the School of Music, Media, and Performance might be more familiar with the techniques of documentary film, for example, than English students. Criminology students might struggle with the lack of empirical material; English students might be confident when analysing poetry, but may be more uncertain than Sociology students when tackling museums and memorials. However, some members of the School regarded the idea of a block seminar as a brazen opportunity for a Holocaust "masterclass," rather than an opportunity to nurture divergent skills bases. This view is at odds with the fact that it is much more difficult to teach students from various disciplines: we could not rely on an equivalent base of previous learning for each seminar. More obviously, it is also difficult sometimes (but also—and often—extremely rewarding) to teach unfamiliar students from a subject area different to that of the tutor's.

One of the most rewarding aspects of teaching the module has been the interdisciplinary nature of the seminar discussions. Most students have commented positively on this experience (91% were satisfied, very satisfied, or extremely satisfied with the module when it first ran in 2004–5, according to the Module Evaluative Questionnaires collected at the end of the semester), but there were significant problems to overcome for certain students in terms of the module design. The Military History (MIL) students in 2004–5 felt particularly embattled, since they were not au fait with some of the basic theoretical, Cultural Studies-based, approaches that were taken in relation to the texts. These students (who seemed unfamiliar with self-reflective texts such as E. H. Carr's *What is History?*) were initially reluctant to begin to think about history as narrative, or queer readings of *Schindler's List*. When one Military History student challenged a Journalism student about his reading of Goethe as a homoeroticized Nazi, the former student burst in tears when the latter defended his position. This proved to be the most uncomfortable moment in the year for the tutors, partly because it illustrated the potential pitfalls of multidisciplinary seminars. The MIL student claimed that no one on the module (including the tutors) had taken the Military History students seriously. Ironically, the MIL recruits were the most articulate and gorgeously opinionated students on the entire module, who initiated extremely sophisticated discussions of memorials, museums, and Art Spiegelman's *Maus* in particular. Indeed, in one *Maus* session, one of the tutors played devil's advocate by suggesting that the comix unfortunately misrepresents history (for example, in relation to the Polish soldiers in Nazi uniform, and the position of the Arbeit Macht Frei gates in Auschwitz): paradoxically, the MIL students were the most vociferous in their defence of *Maus* as an act of secondary witnessing, in which, they argued, historical accuracy might be less important than ethical issues surrounding the artist's proxy-witnessing of Vladek's testimony. Hence the student's response seems to have arisen more particularly from the belief that Military History students have a very different skills base at level three than other students across the School and Faculty at Salford. In 2005–6, due to a clerical error, the module was not offered to MIL students. The seminars between Sociology, English, Criminology, and Journalism students were much less confrontational than in the previous year, yet the tutors secretly admitted that they missed the challenges of teaching more openly multidisciplinary seminars.

Overall, the unfolding of the students' self-conscious engagement with the insights, and limits, that their subject-based knowledge could provide has been the most positive aspect of teaching the module. It could be argued, however, that this self-consciousness is belied by the interdisciplinary limitations of the module. Whilst the module is delivered to various degree programmes, the choice of texts and sessions revolves around a strictly Cultural Studies-orientated remit. Literature, testimony, films, photographs, museums, and memorials feature on a week-by-week basis, but the tutors did not include sessions on, for example, historical narratives, philosophy, and tourism. This is excusable in the sense that such areas do not form the expertise of the tutors involved, whose remit otherwise encompasses Film Studies, Literary Studies, Sociology, Critical Theory, and Criminology. One of the MIL students' criticisms of the module—that it does not include a session specifically on historical narratives—is correct in that a multidisciplinary module could be envisaged with tutors teaching specific sessions from various academic backgrounds (Marcia D. Horn discusses one such module at length in *Teaching the Representation of the Holocaust*).[2] The ensuing problem from our perspective would then be one of coverage: how many disciplines and genres can students come to (some sort of) terms with in eleven weeks? Nevertheless, student expectations are usually high (and often, frankly, unfeasible) in relation to their own subject areas on this module: despite clearly being told in the first lecture that the focus for this module would not be on traditional historical narratives (or on the self-conscious narration of history), some MIL students clearly still expected that Hilberg or Goldhagen would mysteriously materialize in week eleven. Behind these expectations is, perhaps, the presumption that the most important representations of the Holocaust reside in the minds of historians, an assumption which the module challenges. As Eaglestone states in his report on the teaching conference, literary and film texts are "doing something much more than teaching 'history' by another means . . . these texts [stand] in their own right as important artistic events, rather than as illustrations to a historical narrative."[3]

Self-assessment

Apart from the multidisciplinary seminars, the other, most rewarding aspect of the module has been the opportunity to devise, and mark, an innovative form of assessment. As part of the module assessment (worth 25% of the final mark), students are required to write a self-reflective statement of a thousand words. They are expected to comment self-consciously on the composition of their individual project, the module as a whole and (more ambitiously) on the ethics of learning in general. Students complete (an unassessed) mid-semester project proforma, which initiates the process of self-reflexive work. On this form they comment on, amongst other things, why they have chosen their particular area of research (the module has no set essay questions or exam), and are asked to discuss any problems with the primary and secondary materials, or the length and limits of the project. In the final assessment, students are encouraged to write in a more sophisticated manner about the development of the project, the seminar discussions, and their learning in general. For example, they are asked to think about whether their views about the Holocaust have changed since starting the module, whether they found any of the research materials especially troubling, and how representations of violence differ between the various genres taught on the module.[4] The module tutors initially expected the perpetrator images in *Night and Fog* to be the most unsettling, whereas in 2004–5 many students commented that they found the poems the most upsetting material on the module, since they did not feel that this genre—unlike documentary film—should be pertinent to Holocaust representation.[5] A Journalism student commented in their statement that the film images did not disturb some students due to subject-based specialisms: "Looking at some of my classmates' reactions to the images on screen [in *Night and Fog*] was interesting since I did not find the images on display moving at all. Having undertaken a media-based degree programme [I realize that] documentaries have their own agenda and are very manipulative . . . But the English students may have thought the same of me when I was touched by the poetry and prose sessions."[6] Rather than attributing a lack of response to empathy fatigue in general, this student comments on an emotional distancing proportional to familiarity with generic techniques. It is also noteworthy that because students are told in the first session to think about the content of seminar discussions and viewings, and comment on them in the statements if relevant, the students are perhaps more attentive to each other's opinions and reactions in class. Learning becomes part of a genuine group experience, rather than an individual's isolated response to a module in an examination hall.

The students are also asked to think about whether it was difficult to establish critical distance from the project material, the seminar discussions as a whole, and whether (thinking about module design) representations of the Holocaust should be privileged over other historical (or, indeed, contemporary) atrocities. One student commented that they "found it hard when attempting to critically evaluate personal testimonies as I felt that to critique someone's experience of the Holocaust was trivializing their experiences in some way . . . I felt that I was not in a position to criticise their experiences." These comments demonstrate the positive difficulties in teaching testimony. Indeed, the connections between testimony and fiction comprise one of the dialectics that Robert Eaglestone argues in "Teaching Holocaust Writing and Film" are "awaiting working through as research and reflection on Holocaust pedagogy develops and deepens." Students are often loathe to critique (misread sometimes as "criticize") testimonies since it seems tantamount to trivializing lives. In an article prior to the teaching conference, Eaglestone remembers a colleague recalling "her seminar group's shock on hearing her suggest that what had so moved them in a particular Holocaust account was not the events, per se, but the quality of the writing."[7] Instead of critiquing "texts," such students, and the author of this particular statement, believe they are talking and writing directly about "experiences." In 2005–6 one of the tutors introduced Eaglestone's discussion about pleasure and testimony from *The Holocaust and the Postmodern* into the classroom, and was met by a severe reluctance on the students' part to talk about the process of reading testimony that was not in evidence in the sessions on, say, short stories.[8] In contrast, by the end of the course, students frequently wrote in their statements about how they were troubled about having *enjoyed* the module: one wrote in 2005–6 that it "was a refreshing change . . . to feel that this module is a 'refreshing' anything daunts me." Such reflexive moments in seminars on testimony and in the final statements are evidence of the challenges in teaching testimony, and how students (rightly) perceive that there might be different ways in which to read this genre in contrast with fiction and poetry.

Testimony is taught in week two (in relation to Primo Levi): students are already beginning to be self-reflexive about reading practices at this early point in the module. Both tutors point out throughout "Representing the Holocaust" that this process of self-conscious critique is not limited to moments of critical (i.e. academic) reflection, and encourage students to think about the moments when the set authors/directors/artists on the module engage self-referentially with the problems of representation in the primary texts themselves; for example, when Tadeusz Borowski ruminates on the possibility (or not) of an adequate poetry of atrocity in the poem "October Sky." This form of self-reflective assessment was the first of its kind in English at Salford when introduced in 2004, although reflective statements have been utilized in the Salford Politics, Sociology, and History sections for over ten years. All the Politics and History modules now have some form of self-assessment; the first year contains the highest proportion. In contrast, English lags behind other subjects in terms of this kind of assessment. In an English Subject Centre report in 2003 on the various forms of assessment the traditional essay and unseen exam were by far the most popular forms.[9] The self-reflective statement did not even figure in the list, behind peer assessment, vivas, multiple choice tests, and computer-based tests. This may have been an oversight, although student logs (which came tenth out of sixteen varieties) were recognized, which, even if only referring to the progress of a planned presentation, usually contain some form of self-reflection.

The recent rise in popularity in self-reflective statements in English departments is due, no doubt, to the boom in the teaching of creative writing over the last ten years. The self-reflective statement has been central to assessment procedures in this discipline for some time. Not only does it allow students to reflect on creative processess such as editing and composition, it also comprises a creative process in itself. Such statements are a form of poetics, as many practitioners in the field argue, such as the poet and critic Robert Sheppard from Edge Hill University, who has written several editions of his own poetics. In 2003, the English Subject Centre commissioned a report on these "supplementary discourses," which concluded that they are effective because "The students are clear about the reflective functions of the practice of writing about their own work for their own continuing practice. They see that it is part of an ongoing process of reflection, and not simply a retrospective valorisation of their work."[10] In contrast with the teaching of literary and cultural studies, in creative writing there is "already much debate about the nature of the practice of supplementary discourses" (39). Despite the relative paucity of such self-reflective critical assessment on a national scale in the area of literature, we believe that this form of assessment has been extremely successful on "Representing the Holocaust." The External Examiner for English commented in 2006 that the course comprised the most innovative module in the School in terms of its design and assessment. It was "An exemplary module, and an excellent example of an interdisciplinary module."

In Phil Bannister and Ian Baker's report on self assessment in the English Department at Sheffield Hallam University, they conclude that "By becoming more reflective, we believe students are better able to judge the effectiveness of their own performance and become aware of improvement in a particular skill, or set of skills, over time."[11] In relation to the teaching of Holocaust Studies in particular, reflective statements can address what Eaglestone calls the "serious pedagogic questions and problems" which arise in modules where, as he recalls, students can cry in the corridor after reading an account of the Warsaw Ghetto, and shout at each other in class over the significance of historical inaccuracies in *Schindler's List*.[12] Teaching Holocaust literature and film "tends to be full of moments like these." Marianne Hirsch and Irene Kacandes comply with this view when they recall the "most intense, challenging, exhilarating, and painful classroom encounters."[13] Self-reflective statements facilitate the discussion and analysis of such moments and encounters in a way which more traditional forms of assessment do not allow.

Students taking "Representing the Holocaust" are given a series of guidelines and bullet points in the module handbook on how to think about writing such a self-reflective statement. These are meant to be springboards to reflective work rather than a prescriptive series of questions, in contrast with more formalized approaches to self-reflection in other universities, such as the English courses at Sheffield Hallam University, where students are given a self-assessement sheet with boxes for them to comment on the positive and negative aspects of their essays (this mirrors the peer assessment process in creative writing). Many of the English, Journalism, and Criminology students who have not taken any creative writing modules, or come across such statements in other courses (unlike the Politics, Sociology, and History students) are nervous of this form of assessment. Hence, as well as the indicative bullet points in the handbook, a whole session in week twelve is given over to a discussion of how to write self-consciously on critical writing. (This session has the added advantage of drawing students to an important seminar at the end of the module who might otherwise be tempted to miss revision sessions.) As well as discussing the guidelines in the handbook, critical material is also set for that week: Carolyn Dean's essay "Empathy and the Pornography of Suffering" facilitates a discussion about the problems of consuming of cultural artifacts without thinking self-reflectively about the ethics of consumption.[14] Dean's extended critique of the metaphor of pornography in the context of reactions to representations of twentieth-century atrocities leads to a discussion about whether the students have thought about the ethics of learning on this particular module; or, indeed, whether they think such thinking is relevant to the course, or university pedagogy in general. Dean ends her article by stating that the pornography metaphor is ultimately working too hard to encompass every unreflective cosumption of atrocity; critics must try, she argues, to devise a new vocabulary.

The assessment on the module encourages students to attempt to come up with instances of such a vocabulary in relation to Holocaust representation, as well as to register openly limit points when they could not find a suitable discourse, and felt that language somehow defeated them. Many students have written that they had not been made to think about the ethics of learning on any previous module on their degrees. Nevertheless, the overall figure of the student as consumer has reigned supreme in the statements: most think it absolutely appropriate, for example, that they should gain marks for writing about atrocities. However, there is often a concomitant acknowledgement that they still feel uncomfortable about having to articulate how and why they feel uncomfortable about some of the material. (It should be noted that the tutors in no way feel "above" the students' discomfort, since critics in the field of Holocaust Studies very rarely comment self-reflectively themselves on the material they utilize, and how careers are made out of images of atrocity.) Despite what many university managers and administrators might think, students are also usually not enamoured with learning outcomes, so the ability to critique the concept of such utilitarian "outcomes" on this module is often greeted with relish. Of course, many students critique the notion of a utilitarian learning process whilst still, ultimately, upholding their rights to consume the material for their own benefit. Yet such critiques are still ironic, given that the relatively recent notion of "outcomes" was presumably intended to help students with their studies, whereas the most common reaction amongst students looking at learning outcomes on page one of a module handbook in a lecture is to turn surreptitiously to page two. Indeed, many of the government-driven additions to the teaching experience in HE over the last two decades (module handbooks, aims and objectives, learning outcomes, module evaluative questionnaires, discussion of retention rates, and student satisfaction questionnaires, to name but a few) have come at the expense of a discussion about the ethics of learning.[15]

All this focus on pedagogical ethics might suggest, to some, that the module aspires to a dreary post-Adornoian and post-Levinasian view of pedagogy, in which self-consciously agonizing over the ethics of consumption paradoxically gains the students the highest marks. Such a process might seem to be out of kilter with recent developments in (literary) Holocaust Studies, where several critics have attempted to move beyond Adorno's haunting statement in 1949 that "To write poetry after Auschwitz is barbaric," a statement that has been (often problematically) extended to all forms of post-Holocaust culture.[16] Roger Luckhurst has recently critiqued the focus on vexed aesthetics in trauma studies, for example, which leads to what he terms a "trauma knot."[17] One of the module tutors has also recently critiqued the focus on vexed aesthetics in relation to Holocaust and post-Holocaust poetry: the poetry canon has followed a modernist aesthetic by championing the agonized poetics of writers such as Paul Celan and Geoffrey Hill, when, arguably, the testimonial poetics of writers such as Tadeusz Borowski are actually the more innovative artistic form. Most of these developments ask for a reorientation, rather than absolute abandonment, of an ethics of reading, however, and also illustrate that self-conscious critiques of the aesthetic have formed the backbone of much post-Holocaust criticism for the last fifty years or so, and will (justifiably) do so for many years to come.

Hence we think it justifiable that students on this module are asked to think about whether they have particular obligations and responsibilities when taking a course about the Holocaust, particularly when the alternative might be an unreflective learning (or, at best, an unarticulated reflective learning). (The normalized discourse of "taking" a module has interesting connotations in the context of consumerism and an ethics of learning.) The self-reflective statement offers the students an opportunity for an ethical response to such issues of personal responsibility, and engagement with the "other's" experience. Of course, some of the writing in the statements is impressionistic rather than critical (one student "felt a bit of anger in what went on during the Holocaust"), but this can happen in any form of assessment. And rather than fall into a hairshirted critique of their own learning, the students are also encouraged to think about the discourses surrounding an ethics of learning. One of the indicative bullet points in the handbook asks, echoing Gillian Rose, whether it is an instance of "Holocaust piety" to think too self-consciously about self-conscious reponses to Holocaust representation.[18] Quoting a comment from one of Geoffrey Hill's critics in the next bullet point, we ask whether critics and students who always think self-reflexively about such representations risk turning post-Holocaust art into the "gravel of the joyless."[19]

Notes

1. Robert Eaglestone, "Teaching Holocaust Writing and Film" (article subsequent to the conference), www.english.heacademy.ac.uk/explore/ publications/newsletters/newsissue8/eaglestone.html.
2. One of the MIL students commented in the Module Evaluative Questionnaire that they would rather "fry their own testicles" than take this module again; an unfortunate comment given the module's focus on representations of violence.
3. In the module handbook we write about the "queering" of students (since we could think of no better term) through taking on board the facets of unfamiliar disciplines. One MIL student received a third mark when their overall profile was at 2: 1 level: pedagogically, was it a good or bad decision for the student to have taken the module? Good, perhaps, if they appreciated a body of knowledge and critical thinking beyond that required in their own subject area. If learning is about learning about difference, and various critical approaches to an important topic of pedagogy, then perceived threats to knowledge bases (the "other" can threaten, of course, as well as enlighten) can only be a positive outcome. But if learning is about students gaining the highest marks, number crunching, School prizes for the best marks, and the utilitarian outcomes of learning outcomes, then these "threats" are harmful.
4. Some of the most surprising, and troubling, reactions to the question about whether their views had changed about the Holocaust during the

module came from four ERASMUS students from the Czech Republic in 2005–6. (ERASMUS and SOCRATES students have always been attracted to the module in large numbers, perhaps because of the international perspective: they have done presentations on, amongst other things, memorials in The Netherlands, museums in Israel, and testimonies in the Czech language.) One of the Czech students commented that at "high school I had a teacher who was very old and her approaches towards Jews were similar to Hitler's. It could be compared to the proverb 'good Jew is dead Jew.' And that is why I was very influenced by this kind of approach. Now, after the end of the module, I feel ashamed about my approach and my wrong ideas." The ethics of learning can include a self-reflexive approach to anti-Semitic viewpoints, a process that is of course unquantifiable in a final mark, and yet arguably central, in this case, to the learning process. Self-reflective statements are able to pick up on such developments in a way in which traditional assessment procedures cannot. A more troubling response to the module as a whole came from a UK student in 2005–6, who commented (along with a few others in a previous year) that the module was concentrated too much on Jewish survivors and their testimony. The comment is peculiar at best, and, at worst, borders on the anti-Semitic, since there was only one session on testimony (Primo Levi), and (as the tutors point out in the first session), most of the authors/directors/artists on the module (Alain Resnais, Jean Cayrol, Tadeusz Borowski, Claude Lanzmann, the perpetrator photographers, the discussed newsreel editors and museum curators, etc.) are not actually Jewish. The comment thus arises from either a peculiarly blinkered (and ideologically suspect) perspective, or just plain ignorance.

5. The reason for this was usually that they considered poetry to be the most aesthetic of genres, which had, in their view, no place for images of atrocity. Most of the students who commented in this manner were Criminologists, but rather than write off such a perspective, it should be noted how close this conclusion is to Adorno's own concept of "barbaric" poetry (discussed later in this article).
6. Pleasingly, students often surprise themselves in their reactions to unfamiliar genres. One of the Criminology students commented that "The seminar that we had on the poetry of the Holocaust was surprisingly very enjoyable . . . the poetry by Tadeusz Borowski, and the (oral) poem by Paul Celan really stood out as the most memorable and had the most impact of the whole module."
7. www.english.heacademy.ac.uk/explore/publications/newsletters/newsissue7/eaglestone.html.
8. Robert Eaglestone, *The Holocaust and the Postmodern* (Oxford: Oxford University Press, 2004), p. 38.
9. Survey of the English Curriculum and Teaching in UK Higher Education (2003): 38.
10. Scott Thurston and Robert Sheppard, "Supplementary Discourses in Creative Writing Teaching part ii", www.english.heacademy.ac.uk/archive/projects/reports/supdisc_cwrit.doc.

11. Phil Bannister and Ian Baker, *Self Assessment* (Newcastle: University of Northumbria at Newcastle, 2000), p. 7.
12. See note 7.
13. Eds. Marianne Hirsch and Irene Kacandes, *Teaching the Representation of the Holocaust* (New York: The Modern Language Association of America, 2004), p. 7.
14. Carolyn Dean, "Empathy and the Pornography of Suffering," *differences: a Journal of Feminist Cultural Studies*, 14: 1 (2003): 88–124.
15. Students having clearly begun to internalize the discourse of Module Evaluative Questionnaires: one of the statements begins, "I would recommend this course to anyone. . . ." The Salford MEQs are split into two sections: the first one asks the students to evaluate the module themselves; the second one (as, presumably, a quality control) asks whether they would recommend it to a friend. Many of the listed "innovations" in universities over the last twenty years, including MEQs, share a desire to quantify the learning process. As the authors of the project on supplementary discourses gleefully conclude, students "tended to emphasise the function" of the self-reflective statements "for their own self-development. In a world obsessed with measurement (which proposes that you can fatten a pig by measuring it) this is reassuring" (39).
16. Theodor Adorno, "Cultural Criticism and Society," in *Prisms*, trans. S. and S. Weber (London: Neville Spearman, 1967), pp. 17–35, 34.
17. Both the Luckhurst and Rowland articles are due to be published in a future edition of *History and Memory*.
18. Gillian Rose, *Mourning Becomes the Law: Philosophy and Representation* (Cambridge: Cambridge University Press, 1996).
19. James Wood "Too Many Alibis," *London Review of Books*, 1 July 1999: 24–6, 24.

7
Teaching the Holocaust in French Studies: Questions of Mediation and Experience

Ursula Tidd

Since the end of the Second World War, France has had much difficulty confronting the nature of its relationship with Nazism and the Holocaust. During the war France was in the unique and complex position of both collaborating with its Nazi occupiers and being at war with them and then subsequently forming part of the Allied victory over Germany. What Henry Rousso described in 1990 as the "Vichy Syndrome" or the repressed guilt of collaboration at the heart of the French national unconscious has slowly manifested itself and since the 1970s, France has been reassessing its role during the Second World War.[1] A more complex picture of France's Holocaust experience has emerged over the last thirty years or so as a result of various factors. These include: the changed stance on the part of the French government and the Catholic Church in relation to their account of their actions during the Nazi Occupation; the public debate triggered by the release of Claude Lanzmann's *Shoah* (1985) among other Holocaust and Occupation-related films and documents; the prosecution of high profile war crimes trials and libel cases in France during the 1980s and 1990s, the challenge to the post-war Gaullist construction of France as a nation of resisters and its consequent mythification of France's wartime record, the public and legal condemnations of Holocaust negationists and the impact of the commemoration of events relating to the Holocaust and the Second World War.

The evolving discourse concerning France's relationship to Nazism and its role in the Holocaust is clearly germane to and reflected in the design of school and university French studies curricula both within and beyond France. In France, for example, it was not until the 1970s that the Nazi genocide of the Jews was added to the secondary school curriculum and it was only included in the *baccalauréat* programme as recently as 1983.[2] Within the discipline of French studies in the UK higher education sector, undergraduate students usually have a general knowledge of the historical background to the Nazi Occupation of France during the Second World War from broad-based first year history courses at university or from prior AS/A2 study. However, at first year level and sometimes beyond, they are often not very familiar with French Holocaust culture. In French studies university departments nationally, many have one or several option courses covering historical, cultural, and political aspects of the Second World War. These are often packaged as relating to Vichy or Occupied France rather than to the Holocaust per se and, in the last twenty years with the increased scholarly interest in memory studies, now have a sharper focus on the memorial and historiographical aspects of the period.

Since 2001, I have taught an MA course unit in French Studies at the University of Manchester entitled "Trauma and Memory in Twentieth Century French Life Writing." In addition to a general French history course in the first year, students can also choose a final year undergraduate two-semester option entitled "Occupied France" that includes study of a Holocaust text, Jorge Semprún's *Le Grand Voyage* (1963), alongside Resistance novels and plays, such as Vercors's *Le Silence de la Mer* (1942) and Jean-Paul Sartre's *Huis Clos* (1944) and *Les Mouches* (1943), and a fascist novel by Pierre Drieu La Rochelle, *Gilles* (1939).[3] The aims of this final year undergraduate option are to explore the political and social causes and effects of the German defeat and Occupation of France and to analyse a range of ideologically motivated literary responses to the experience of the Second World War. It consistently recruits very well at final year level and is taught through a combination of lectures on the relevant historical background, the viewing of archive film footage, seminar discussion, and enquiry-based learning activities in which students pursue their own research tasks with supervision from the tutor. Some students have pursued their interest in Holocaust writing developed in this final year course option by choosing the MA course option on "Trauma and Memory."

The idea for the postgraduate course originated in a cluster of longer term research interests. For most of the 1990s, I conducted research and published mainly in the area of Simone de Beauvoir studies, specifically on her autobiographical writings and philosophy. A predominating interest in this respect was the politics and functions of testimony and truth telling in autobiographical writing, specifically within the post-war French context. I was also interested in the broader questions relating to how literature might represent or at least engage with traumatic experiences and limit experiences more generally, especially in terms of literature's relationship to historiography and the phenomenological significance of the event. The Second World War and its aftermath is a major preoccupation in Beauvoir's autobiography, fiction, and philosophical and political writing. Moreover, in addition to being a close associate of Claude Lanzmann, she wrote the preface to the screenplay of *Shoah* and to Jean-François Steiner's 1966 book on the Jewish resistance in Treblinka, and has authored other short Holocaust-related texts.[4] I subsequently broadened my research interests to include the writing of French Holocaust survivors, retaining these general areas of focus. In 2001, I taught the MA course, "Trauma and Memory in Twentieth Century French Life Writing" for the first time, initially as part of a broader, pre-existing MA programme on "Cultures of Transgression." As the title of the course suggests, the focus was on the representation and transmission of traumatic experience in Holocaust autobiographical writing. The aim, then, was to explore how individual and collective memories might be inscribed and to analyse the various modes of testimony in operation in four rather different autobiographical presentations of Holocaust experience.

The selection of primary texts entailed opting for more or less well-known figures and texts in the French Holocaust literary canon namely, Charlotte Delbo, Georges Perec, Marguerite Duras, and Jorge Semprún, mainly because of students' relative lack of familiarity with French Holocaust literature at undergraduate level. In my experience, students are usually unfamiliar with Delbo and Semprún's writing; have "heard of" Duras and Perec and often have read another work by Duras.

The texts chosen can be considered to belong to what Lawrence Langer has described as the second of two phases of response to the

Holocaust, that is a phase marked by a predominant focus on memory, in which—as he writes—we are "moving from what we know of the event (the province of historians), to how to remember it, which shifts the responsibility to our own imaginations and what we are prepared to admit there."[5] The set texts were also chosen because they foreground in various ways the problematics of memorial inscription and the literarity of the enterprise as conceived and, in so doing, engage creatively with testimony and the autobiographical genre more broadly. The texts span a period of twenty-five years, starting with Delbo's *Aucun de nous ne reviendra*, published in 1970, the first volume in her Holocaust trilogy, *Auschwitz et après*. Delbo, whose work is translated and hence quite well known in Holocaust studies, was a Communist Resistance fighter who was in imprisoned in France in 1942, then sent to Auschwitz and Ravensbrück. The particular areas of Delbo's writing that are explored in seminar discussion are her notions of the different forms of memory (deep or traumatic memory; common memory; external or intellectual memory; sense memory) in relation to the possibilities of testimony, the intercalation of prose and poetry in terms of the functions of language and the representation of Holocaust experience, and the specificity of women's Holocaust experience. Delbo's political trajectory, her analyses of how experience is memorially inscribed and her creative engagement with literary genre link her with the last writer studied, Jorge Semprún. Both Semprún and Delbo are presenting first-hand accounts of Holocaust experience as political prisoners, and both are highly literary writers who probe the parameters of language, representation and testimony. In *L'Ecriture ou la vie* (1994), Semprún engages precisely with the difficulties of imagining, understanding and remembering Holocaust experience, foregrounding the importance of "artifice" and literariness in his testimonial task. Stylistic considerations are crucial, according to the narrator of *L'Ecriture ou la vie*, in order that the Holocaust narrative might find an audience:

> I start to doubt the possibility of telling the story. Not that what we lived through is indescribable. It was unbearable, which is something else entirely (that won't be hard to understand), something that doesn't concern the form of a possible account, but its substance. Not its articulation, but its density. The only ones who will

manage to reach this substance, this transparent density, will be those able to shape their evidence into an artistic object, a space of creation. Or of re-creation. Only the artifice of a masterly narrative will prove capable of conveying some of the truth of such testimony.[6]

As Ofelia Ferrán has argued, in his bid to communicate the event to future generations of readers Semprún illustrates certain of Paul Ricoeur's claims in *Temps et récit* concerning the mutual dependence of history and fiction as narrative forms that both rely upon imagination and memory to evoke the *tremendum horrendum*.[7] A Spanish Francophone writer who has written many of his Holocaust texts in French, Semprún frequently draws upon a wealth of French, Spanish, and German cultural and philosophical references, and reflects on the philosophical aspects and linguistic pragmatics of representing Holocaust experience in these languages. Semprún invites his readers to question the parameters of what constitutes a specifically *French* Holocaust experience. The multilingualism of his texts, which is closely connected to his experience of political exile in 1936 from Franco's Spain, presents Semprún's Holocaust experience as a *European* rather than a specifically Spanish or French phenomenon. Hence, an issue that is raised here is to what extent memorial inscriptions are inflected by interplays of national and supra-national identities, evident in Semprún's multilingualism and philosophical and literary intertextuality. As Marianne Hirsch and Irene Kacandes note, in Holocaust studies, "teachers have to confront issues of language, translation and translatability. Surely internment in Nazi concentration camps counts as one of the most multilingual experiences of the twentieth century."[8] Teaching Semprún's Holocaust writing entails a consideration of such multilingualism and translatability in the mediation of Holocaust experience, as well as the question of the linguistic mediation of the traumatic event more generally to be addressed in a consideration of any Holocaust text. Moreover, Semprún's writing raises yet other issues in this respect concerning the construction of identity in exile and diaspora as represented in Holocaust cultural forms, now that debates move beyond some of the questions addressed during the 1990s, one of which has been identified by James E. Young, as a tendency "to locate literary responses to the Holocaust in the national communities that spawned them."[9]

The other two texts studied, Perec's *W ou le souvenir d'enfance* (1975) and Duras's *La Douleur* (1985) constitute a rather more tangential engagement with Holocaust experience. Both are major writers in the post-war French canon, linked at various stages in their careers with avant-gardist literary movements. In *W ou le souvenir d'enfance*, in two parallel narratives which initially seem to have little in common but eventually converge on the image of the concentration camp, Perec engages through allegory and iconography with his family experience of the Holocaust, especially that of his mother who died in Auschwitz. Perec has been described by Susan Rubin Suleiman as belonging to the "1.5 generation" of Holocaust survivors, defined as "child survivors of the Holocaust, too young to have had an adult understanding of what was happening to them but old enough to have been there during the Nazi persecution of Jews."[10] The inclusion of Perec's text therefore introduces the question of the Holocaust's generational impact and of the parameters of "postmemory."[11] Duras, however, in *La Douleur*, testifies as a witness to another's survival, namely that of Robert Antelme, her first husband imprisoned as a Communist first in Gandersheim then in Dachau. In so doing, Duras explores the roles of suffering, amnesia, and memory in survival. In common with the other set texts, *La Douleur* confounds generic identities, poses an epistemological challenge to the question of survival, both in the case of the narrating "I" and of Robert L. who is anticipated to return. Echoing earlier Durassian concerns, *La Douleur* is constructed around a metaphysical void; a textual universe in which (self-)dispossession and abandonment predominate and witnessing and forgetting shade into one another.

All of these texts consequently explore different approaches to testifying to Holocaust experience and the narrators concerned position themselves somewhat differently, which raises interesting questions with regard to ownership and testimonial authority of autobiographical experience—an issue especially acute in terms of the Holocaust in the context of Primo Levi's claim that the true witnesses are the "sommersi", those who did not survive.

The course is organized into six one-hour sessions which take place during a single semester, the first and last sessions being ones in which introductory and general theoretical issues relating to all four texts are explored. Each of the remaining four sessions focuses on a particular text, although students are strongly encouraged to read as much as they can of the writer's corpus. At Manchester, the MA option courses are designed to interleave with a core critical theory course. Students often draw on their option course texts in their theory course work and they are expected to use theoretical approaches in their option course work. To complement their background in general theory acquired on the core course covering some of the main theoretical approaches, they are provided with additional references in Holocaust and trauma theory. The course is then assessed by one 4,000-word essay, titles of which are set by me or students can suggest one of their own with my approval.

In terms of the student responses to the course so far, one perceived strength identified by students is its delivery exclusively via seminar discussion and student presentations which, it was claimed, helped them think through the sensitive material and questions covered. This dialogic approach was judged to have engaged them more than a lecture-led delivery. That said, as one student observed, it made them also more acutely aware of the "heavy moral responsibility" in talking about the Holocaust and produced an anxiety over how indeed to talk about it at all. In this sense, the silence and fragmented quality of the texts studied can appear to become reinscribed to some degree in the dynamics of seminar interaction. As one student explained: "when talking about such dreadful events this is a potentially difficult situation to be in as one obviously wants to avoid saying anything trite or insincere."[12] This anxiety seems also to reflect a concern over the danger of a possible appropriation of Holocaust experience and over who has authority to speak about it. These are also concerns that are explored in the texts studied. Semprún, for example, echoing Primo Levi, talks in *Le Mort qu'il faut* (2001) about the true witnesses as being those who went to the limit of the experience and hence have not survived and cannot now speak. Given the small number of students taking the course, as numbers are spread across a large range of options, the discussion-led delivery seemed to both help and hinder their participation in the sense that it heightened their responsibility to participate but, in some cases, made it less intimidating, because of the small group size, for them to do so. One student observed that being taught in a small group obliged him to engage with the issues that otherwise he might have been tempted to shy away from or ignore.[13]

A further significant issue is that of the impact on students of reading the set texts in a non-native language, which may produce a distancing effect depending on their particular experience of second language acquisition. María Angélica Semilla Durán has noted more generally in an interesting discussion of Semprún's use of language that bilingualism and multilingualism entail complex processes of psychic adaptation.[14] Second language acquisition and "code-switching"—as the shift from one language to another within the same speech exchange is known in linguistics—entail, according to Durán, the formation of additional mnemonic strata which in turn require the retranslation of pre-existing psychic representations such as the drives, reality, and the law into the new "code." In the Freudian reading of Semprún's bilingualism explored, although the native language usually functions as an ego defence mechanism and the second language as the fragment against which the defence operates, the rhetorical disturbance in Semprún's use of Spanish and French suggests to Durán that this relationship is reversed.[15] In its usual functioning, this implies that there may also be a psychic resistance operant in a bilingual situation such as that of reading texts in a second language that can distance the reader, depending on their experience of second language acquisition. Added to this possible "resistance" is the potentially disidentificatory effect of reading about a traumatic experience that one has not had—assuming that trauma can be recollected and represented at all, which is a complex debate beyond the remit of this discussion.[16] This is not to suggest that one has to have had an experience to be able to respond to its recollection by another person. Indeed, Susan Rubin Suleiman has argued that:

> we all project ourselves into what we read, especially into narrative. Just as it has been claimed that all writing . . . is in some way autobiographical, so it can be claimed that all reading is . . . To recognise aspects of one's own life story in another's is no doubt easier for one who has undergone some of the same experiences, in the same time and the same place; but it would be far too restrictive, and wrongheaded, to suggest that *only* one who has undergone a certain experience can respond to another's story, and to its telling, "properly"—or in my terms, autobiographically. For one thing, no individual's experience of an event, even of the exact same event, is fully identical to another's; even in such a case, it requires an imaginative leap to read the other's story "as if it were one's own". The willingness or ability to make that

imaginative leap may be stronger in one who has firsthand experience of the time and the place; but paradoxically, the closeness to the experience may also provoke a reverse reaction, a refusal to read autobiographically, or to read at all ... the ways of the imagination and its relation to the experience of the self are too complicated for categorical pronouncements.[17]

Having shared an experience may not be especially useful, then, in facilitating an autobiographical response (in Suleiman's terms) to Holocaust writing. However, if one considers the possible effects of psychic resistance that may be entailed in reading in a second language and the problematics of reading about traumatic events—which will trigger different responses in different readers—the "imaginative leap" required may seem considerable. Alternatively, any possible resistance entailed in reading a Holocaust text in a second language may counteract a possible over-identification on the part of the reader and the emotional and empathic unsettlement entailed—especially pertinent perhaps in the case of reading firsthand testimonies because of their heightened potential for provoking "autobiographical reading."

In terms of my own reflections on teaching this MA course, I am aware that, as Semprún notes, I am participating in the proliferation of academic narratives about the Holocaust perhaps at the expense of direct testimonial accounts, both that of the students and of the writers themselves.[18] Perhaps to some degree this is inevitable in a pedagogical context, although a possible response to this concern would be to facilitate further reflection on the part of the students in relation to their own experience of reading these texts. This could entail setting assessment tasks such as a self-reflective commentary or a course diary. Additionally, enabling students to have direct access to different forms of survivors' testimony, either by the explicit incorporation of video testimonies or by the participation of survivors themselves would shift the focus of the course from more abstract theoretical issues concerning testimony and trauma in Holocaust autobiographies to a sharper, less mediated focus on the diversity and nature of Holocaust experience.

In terms of future pedagogical plans, I intend to introduce a final year undergraduate course in 2006–07 which focuses on Holocaust representation in filmic and literary texts, which will include Claude

Lanzmann's *Shoah*, Alain Resnais's *Nuit et Brouillard* (1956) and Elie Wiesel's *La Nuit* (1958). This new course will serve to expand the focus on French Holocaust experience in the undergraduate curriculum and further explore the modes in which that experience might be represented.

Notes

1. Henry Rousso, *Le Syndrome de Vichy* (Paris: Seuil, 1987–1990); *The Vichy Syndrome* (Cambridge: Harvard University Press, 1991).
2. Samuel Totten, "Holocaust Education in Europe" in Walter Lacqueur (ed.) *The Holocaust Encyclopedia* (New Haven and London: Yale University Press, 2001), pp. 301–05 (p. 304).
3. Julie Lawton teaches this course unit.
4. Simone de Beauvoir, "La Mémoire de l'horreur" in Claude Lanzmann, *Shoah* (Paris: Fayard, 1985), pp. 7–10; "Préface" in Jean-François Steiner, *Treblinka* (Paris: Fayard, 1966).
5. Lawrence Langer, *Admitting the Holocaust, Collected Essays* (Oxford, OUP, 1995), p. 13.
6. Jorge Semprún, *L'Ecriture ou la vie*, trans. Linda Coverdale, *Literature or Life* (Harmondsworth: Penguin, 1997), p. 13.
7. Ofelia Ferrán, "'Quanto más escribo, más me queda por decir': Memory, Trauma and Writing in the Work of Jorge Semprún", *MLN* 116 (2001), 266–94, see especially p. 277 and pp. 281–2.
8. Marianne Hirsch and Irene Kacandes, "Introduction" in Hirsch and Kacandes (eds) *Teaching the Representation of the Holocaust* (New York: Modern Language Association of America, 2004), p. 24.
9. James E. Young, "Literature" in Walter Lacqueur (ed.) *The Holocaust Encyclopedia* (New Haven and London: Yale University Press, 2001), pp. 393–98 (p. 398).
10. Susan Rubin Suleiman, "The 1.5 Generation: Georges Perec's *W or the Memory of Childhood*" in Hirsch and Kacandes (eds) *Teaching the Representation of the Holocaust*, pp. 372–85 (p. 372).
11. See Helen Epstein's *Children of the Holocaust: Conversations with Sons and Daughters of Survivors* (New York: Putnam, 1979) and Marianne Hirsch's *Family Frames: Photography, Narrative and Postmemory* (Cambridge: Harvard UP, 1997) for discussion of the phenomenon of "postmemory."
12. Robert Gillan, course feedback.
13. Robert Gillan, course feedback.
14. María Angélica Semilla Durán, *Le Masque et le masqué, Jorge Semprún et les abîmes de la mémoire* (Toulouse: Presses universitaires du Mirail, 2005), p. 234.
15. Semilla Durán, pp. 234–5.
16. See, for example, Cathy Caruth (ed.) *Trauma, Explorations in Memory* (Baltimore and London: The John Hopkins University Press, 1995) and

Unclaimed Experience: Trauma, Narrative and History (Baltimore and London: The John Hopkins University Press, 1996); Shoshana Felman and Dori Laub, *Testimony: Crises of Witnessing in Literature, Psychoanalysis and History* (London: Routledge: 1992); Dominick LaCapra, *Writing History, Writing Trauma* (Baltimore and London: The John Hopkins University Press, 2001).
17. Susan Rubin Suleiman, "War Memories, On Autobiographical Reading" in Lawrence D. Kritzman (ed.) *Auschwitz and After, Race, Culture, and "the Jewish Question" in France* (London and New York: Routledge, 1995), p. 48 and pp. 51–52.
18. Jorge Semprún, *Le Mort qu'il faut* (Paris: Gallimard, 2001), p. 16.

8
History, Memory, Fiction in French Cinema

Libby Saxton

"Is there a relation between trauma and pedagogy?" asks Shoshana Felman. "Can trauma *instruct* pedagogy, and can pedagogy shed light on the mystery of trauma?"[1] The affirmative response anticipated by her questions takes the form of an essay, framed as a "life-testimony," about her experience of teaching a graduate course on literature and testimony. Felman describes how towards the end of the course, a screening of a videotaped Holocaust testimony unexpectedly precipitated a "trauma" or "crisis" in her students which "unwittingly enacted" the class's subject-matter, and had to be contained and reintegrated "in a transformed frame of meaning" through reflection, discussion and writing or "testimony." One of the lessons she draws from this experience is pedagogical: "teaching in itself, teaching as such, takes place precisely only through a crisis: if teaching does not hit upon some sort of crisis, if it does not encounter either the vulnerability or the explosiveness of a (explicit or implicit) critical and unpredictable dimension, it has perhaps *not truly taught*."[2]

When I first read Felman's essay, as a final-year undergraduate contemplating the possibility of future graduate study and teaching, I found some of her conclusions troubling, if not downright alarming. I was disturbed by the parallels she draws between the role of the teacher and the psychoanalyst, and doubted that graduate research would equip me to deal with the fallout of a "crisis" of the kind she describes. More fundamentally, I wondered whether educators have a right, let alone a responsibility, to actively seek to access such crises or traumas in the classroom, and what impact this might have upon the relationship of trust between student and teacher. On more than one level, Felman's argument seemed to challenge traditional conceptions of pedagogical ethics. Rereading the essay eight years on, having taught courses on Holocaust-related material for three years, I retain some of my initial reservations, but find myself more receptive to her claim that the encounter between student, teacher, and text must unsettle and disorientate in order to transform. More forcefully than many other texts, Holocaust representations call into question students' and teachers' preexisting conceptual frameworks, shaking our assumptions about the ways in which knowledge is constructed and transmitted and compelling us to reconsider the relationship between affect and analysis as well as the ethical and pedagogical value of each.

This essay explores some of the specific challenges involved in teaching filmic representations of the Holocaust, focusing in particular on Alain Resnais's *Nuit et brouillard* (*Night and Fog*, 1955) and Claude Lanzmann's *Shoah* (1985). It draws on my experience of teaching an MA course on history and memory in French cinema in the Centre for Film Studies at Queen Mary, University of London.[3] This experience is limited and the essay does not purport to offer a model of exemplary practice. More modestly, it suggests ways in which such films might be approached in class and reflects on questions that have arisen in this context. It is revealing that the "crisis" described by Felman erupted on the first occasion when her students were confronted with visually-mediated, as opposed to literary, testimony. The apparent capacity of visual representations to make historical events more real, tangible, and immediately accessible to students than written ones, particularly in an increasingly image-saturated and visually-literate culture, may account in part for the regularity with which Holocaust educators have recourse to visual resources. A significant proportion of the growing number of courses on the Holocaust in UK universities involve the study of films of various kinds. Relatively few, however, accord them the status of primary object of study; films or film excerpts are often incorporated as sources of information or illustration, as supplements, for example, to historical accounts or literary testimonies. Judith Doneson is critical of what she perceives as a tendency to misuse films as "authentic representations" in such contexts, arguing that they should properly be used instead "to understand the process and function of recreating history through film."[4] Lamenting the rarity of syllabi focusing specifically on the Holocaust and cinema, not least within Film Studies departments, Terri Ginsberg insists, moreover, that an engagement with contemporary film theory is conducive to "a thoroughgoing Holocaust film criticism."[5]

While the objectives and scope of my own course differ significantly from those of the course outlined by Ginsberg in her article, it seeks in distinctive ways to redress aspects of the curricular neglect to which she and Doneson allude. "History, Memory, Fiction in French Cinema" has a double aim: firstly, to introduce students to a spectrum of French films which offer innovative representations of processes of memory and historical traumas; and secondly, to investigate the contribution of these films to current debates about the relations between history, fiction, and testimony. The course was designed as part of an MA in Film Studies but is also available as an option to students on other MA programmes. It attracts participants with undergraduate degrees in a range of disciplines, including Modern Languages, English, History, Geography, and Politics as well as Film Studies. Since all of the set films are available in subtitled versions and much of the assigned reading is in English, a knowledge of French is not a prerequisite. However, students without previous experience of studying cinema are expected to familiarize themselves with basic aspects of the language and theory of film, an understanding of which enriches their analyses of the films.

A brief overview of the course as a whole will provide a context for more detailed discussion of two of the Holocaust films which occupy a central position in the syllabus. We begin by examining a selection of films that challenge conventional understandings of processes of remembrance and forgetting. Agnès Varda's *Sans toit ni loi* (*Vagabond*, 1985) and *Jacquot de Nantes* (1991) and Resnais's *L'Année dernière à Marienbad* (*Last Year at Marienbad*, 1961) employ a range of experimental techniques to explore the formation and transmission of personal memories. Questions of trauma and history are introduced through analysis of Resnais's *Hiroshima mon amour* (1959) and Chris Marker's *La Jetée* (*The Pier*, 1962), which investigate the unpredictable and disruptive resurgence of traumatic memories. These five films are used to facilitate discussion of the specificity of the cinematic medium as a vector of memory, while interdisciplinary supporting literature introduces critical and theoretical frameworks within which this might be conceptualized.[6] The rest of the course develops these preliminary lines of enquiry and initiates others through consideration of representations of specific historical traumas. *Nuit et brouillard* and *Shoah* interrogate the possibilities and limits of the cinematic image as witness to the unprecedented violence of the Holocaust. Resnais's and Lanzmann's films and a series of divergent readings of them are studied alongside the more audience-friendly version of history fabricated by Radu Mihaileanu in his tragi-comedy *Train de vie* (*Train of Life*, 1998) and Slavoj Žižek's critical take on what he dubs "camp comedies."[7] Viewed and read in parallel, these films and texts introduce students to key ideas in ongoing debates about representational limits, the relationship between ethics and aesthetics and the singular properties and potentialities of film as a vehicle of testimony. The final section of the course addresses the contribution of French cinema to the construction of national memory and the exposure of collective amnesia, particularly in relation to the still contested memory of *les années noires*, or the Occupation during the Second World War. Marcel Ophuls's *Le Chagrin et la pitié* (*The Sorrow and the Pity*, 1971), Louis Malle's *Lacombe, Lucien* (1974), Jacques Audiard's *Un héros très discret* (*A Self-Made Hero*, 1996) and Bertrand Tavernier's *Laissez-passer* (*Safe Conduct*, 2001) are considered in the context of debates in historiography and film criticism.[8] These films allude to the Nazis' attempt to annihilate the European Jewry with varying degrees of explicitness, while foregrounding nationally-specific concerns about French collaboration with this policy and what has been called *résistancialisme*, or the Gaullist myth of a nation united in resistance. (I have sometimes varied the filmic corpus to incorporate representations pertaining to other traumatic episodes in recent French history, such as Resnais's *Muriel, ou le temps d'un retour* (*Muriel, or the Time of Return*, 1963) or Tavernier's *La Guerre sans nom* (*The Undeclared War*, 1992), which deal with the troubled legacy of the Franco-Algerian war.)

Of all the films studied on the course, *Nuit et brouillard* and *Shoah* have consistently provoked the most dynamic and engaged seminar discussions, prompted the most sophisticated and self-conscious oral and written responses from students and proved the most difficult—if also the most rewarding—to teach. However, while both films have acquired canonical status and are screened in whole or part in courses on the Holocaust in many different disciplines, little has been written about the singular pedagogical challenges they pose to teachers.[9] *Nuit et brouillard* and *Shoah* have both been heralded as redefining the parameters of Holocaust representation and remain important points of reference in current debates on this subject. In recent years the idea that the reality of the camps is beyond representation and the concomitant notions that it remains "unspeakable", "unimaginable" or "unfathomable" have been treated with growing suspicion. In the wake of interventions by Gillian Rose, Giorgio Agamben, Jacques Rancière, Georges Didi-Huberman, Jean-Luc Nancy and others, rhetorics of "ineffability" are rapidly losing critical currency.[10] Concerns about representability also lie at the heart of the ongoing dispute between Lanzmann and Jean-Luc Godard about the testimonial value and ethical import of archive images of the camps. While Lanzmann dismisses them as "images without imagination," according to Godard, whose celebrated eight-hour video-essay *Histoire(s) du cinéma* (1988–98), like *Nuit et brouillard*, includes a number of images of this kind, they can have, on the contrary, a redemptive function.[11] The differences between the two directors and the controversial photographic exhibition held in Paris in 2001, "Mémoire des camps: photographies des camps de concentration et d'extermination nazis (1933–1999)" ("Memory of the Camps: Photographs of the Nazi Concentration and Extermination Camps (1933–1999)"), have provoked heated discussions in recent French scholarship about the role of the image as witness, including polarized contributions from Didi-Huberman and Gérard Wajcman.[12] My course revisits *Nuit et brouillard* and *Shoah* in the light of these illuminating recent developments, some of which have been largely overlooked in Anglo-American scholarship to date, and which facilitate questioning of the discourses of "unrepresentability" with which both films have been associated.

While teaching typically takes the form of group discussions, often led by students, prior to the screening of *Nuit et brouillard* I deliver a short lecture introducing key concepts and arguments in the debates outlined above to contextualize analysis of the two films. All of the set films (with the exception of *Shoah*, for reasons discussed below) are initially viewed in communal screenings held in the departmental cinema.[13] Such an arrangement has a number of obvious advantages: viewers situated in a darkened room in front of a large screen develop a different relation to the images unfolding before them from viewers watching the same images on a small monitor, who are able to manipulate the duration of the film and more likely to miss those telltale details that are only just visible on the cinema screen (such as the famously censored *képi* in *Nuit et brouillard*). While most screenings are followed by a preliminary discussion of the film, I have found—through trial and error—that this is simply not possible after Resnais's documentary, for reasons anticipated in Felman's account of her students' responses to video testimony. Students are invited instead to spend some time in silence reflecting in writing on their affective, intellectual, and moral responses to the film and formulating ideas in preparation for later discussion.

In the subsequent seminar we review selected excerpts and consider, first of all, how the different components of the film interact to produce meaning. *Nuit et brouillard* has four principal components: black-and-white photographs and film footage from the archive are interpolated with freshly-shot colour images of the camps and accompanied by a voice-over commentary written by the survivor Jean Cayrol and a musical score by Hanns Eisler. Unlike the vast majority of documentaries on the subject of the camps, however, Resnais's incessantly interrogates the relationship between its visual and aural elements and the historical reality they purport to represent, registering doubts about its capacity to render the Holocaust visible, graspable, or knowable. As Leo Bersani and Ulysse Dutoit have noted, our vision is constantly disturbed and disoriented by the dissonant relations between voice, music, and image, which prevent us from becoming absorbed in what we see: "to watch this film is to be turned away from it."[14] This dissonance and its disconcerting effects upon the viewer can be highlighted through a comparison with excerpts from a documentary such as James Moll's *The Last Days* (1998), where images, words and other sounds tend instead to follow a seamless logic of corroboration.

Close attention to specific segments of Resnais's disjunctive montage offers one way of broaching broader questions about the adequacy or legitimacy of different representational strategies. Questions of this kind are unfamiliar to some students; many are more accustomed to studying film from primarily formal or historical perspectives. Preparatory reading for the seminar includes extracts from writings by Saul Friedländer and Berel Lang, which introduce concepts of representational limits, as well as an essay by Charles Krantz which addresses *Nuit et brouillard*'s universalizing, dehistoricizing rhetoric and Resnais's failure to bear witness to the specificity of the fate of Jews.[15] In addition, texts by Didi-Huberman, Joshua Hirsch, and Emma Wilson alert students to the dearth of images depicting the machinery of mass murder in action and explore the documentary, testimonial, and metonymic status of the abundant images taken by the Allies as the camps were liberated.[16] While most of the harrowing archive images of emaciated, traumatized survivors and decomposing corpses recycled by Resnais belong to this latter category, there is one exception. *Nuit et brouillard* and *The Last Days* both include one of the four photographs taken by members of a *Sonderkommando* in and around the gas chamber in Crematorium V at Auschwitz in August 1944. Students are supplied with reproductions of the original image and invited to consider how this exceptional document is recontextualized within each film. The photograph in question shows bodies being burnt in an open-air ditch, though in the version used by Moll and Resnais the doorframe that featured prominently in the original has been excised and, with it, the visible signs of the resourcefulness and courage of the photographer hiding in the gas chamber. However, whereas in *The Last Days* the photograph functions straightforwardly as documentary evidence of the events described by the witnesses, Resnais's montage discourages us from viewing such images as transparent windows onto history. As the camera tracks through empty barracks in Birkenau, Cayrol's commentary warns us that the reality of the camps is "hard for us to uncover traces of now" and remains incommensurable with words and images: "no description, no image can restore their true dimension." We discuss *Nuit et brouillard*'s precarious relation to historical reality in the light of Wilson's argument that Resnais's film may have more in common with Lanzmann's than is often acknowledged by commentators.

A further excerpt serves simultaneously to consolidate and conclude discussion of *Nuit et brouillard* and to provide a point of departure for analysis of *Shoah*. In what students often describe as the most devastating scene of the film, and one that might be viewed as emblematic of his project, Resnais's camera enters a gas chamber at Majdanek. His mobile, exploratory camerawork implies a residual corporeal presence in the desolate, silent chamber, ghosting the passage and perspective of those who died there. As the camera pans across the rough, pitted ceiling, we strain to discern what the commentary identifies as the sole remaining physical traces of human presence: the marks made in the concrete by the fingernails of the dying. Wilson's observation that "the relation between the human markings and the atrocity to which they bear witness, and of which they offer material proof, challenges rationality and sense-making," and Hirsch and Vincent Lowy's comments on the missing image of death in the gas chamber provide valuable prompts for analysis of this scene.[17] We discuss, furthermore, the extent to which the form and content of sequences such as this render the traditional tools of critical analysis inadequate or inappropriate—a question which is also pertinent to *Shoah*.

The nine-and-a-half hours of Lanzmann's filmic meditation on memory, testimony, and annihilation present a distinct set of challenges to students and teachers. The most obvious and immediate of these relates to its sheer length, which makes a communal screening of the film in its entirety impractical. Nevertheless, viewers can gain only a limited understanding of *Shoah*'s complex circular architecture, its expansive scope and its strategic omissions and blind spots from excerpts alone. By way of a compromise, students on the course view the first two hours as a group in the cinema and the rest elsewhere in their own time. Their initial reactions to the film, prior to digesting the assigned reading, are eclectic and often enlightening. While some describe becoming utterly absorbed in Lanzmann's relentless pursuit of truth, others acknowledge resistance to—even impatience with—the slow pace of his montage, his insistence on apparently insignificant details and his understated visuals. *Shoah* consists principally of interviews with survivors, perpetrators, and bystanders intercut with present-day images of the killing sites. But what is arguably most challenging about the film is what Lanzmann chooses not to show. Not only does he refuse to reconstruct the past in the manner of other filmmakers studied on the course; he also eschews archive footage. *Shoah* consistently avoids direct images of the catastrophic event named in its title.

Certain excerpts from the film are reviewed in seminars to facilitate evaluation of this lacuna.[18] An early sequence shows the survivor Simon Srebnik roaming around the grassy clearing in the Chelmno forest which he recognizes as the place where bodies were unloaded from gas vans and incinerated, but where all that remains of the furnaces are nondescript, harmless-looking foundations. The non-coincidence between word and image, between the atrocities described by the witness and the deceptive serenity of the landscape makes manifest and tangible the progressive disappearance of traces which Lanzmann identifies as the point of departure for his film.[19] Particularly illuminating with regard to questions of representability and ineffability is the much-discussed scene where Abraham Bomba, a former member of the Treblinka *Sonderkommando*, is urged by Lanzmann to imitate the physical actions he performed under duress in the camp in a rented barber's shop in Tel Aviv. As he remembers the arrival of a transport of women from his home town, Czestochowa, Bomba falls silent, stops working and turns away from the camera, which promptly zooms in closer until his face fills almost the entire screen. Ignoring Bomba's request that they interrupt the interview, Lanzmann repeatedly urges him to keep going, but it is nearly three-and-a-half minutes before Bomba is ready and able to pick up his story. This elaborately staged scene prompts debate about the ethics of Lanzmann's treatment of his interviewees. While some students are uncomfortable with his tendency to manipulate the witnesses, to channel their testimonies through his own point of view and to continue filming even when this appears to be against their wishes, others argue that his ends justify his means, even on the occasions when these involve forms of subterfuge. The form and content of Bomba's testimony can also productively be contrasted with those of another cinematic scene depicting Jewish women in what we are led to believe is a gas chamber: the controversial shower room sequence in Steven Spielberg's *Schindler's List* (1993).

While comparisons of this kind can bring into focus the ethical dimensions of competing representational strategies, supporting texts warn students to be cautious about simple binary oppositions between *Shoah* and *Schindler's List* of the sort posited by Lanzmann.[20] Students are provided with an annotated select bibliography which aims to assist them in finding their way around the ever-growing interdisciplinary body of writings devoted to *Shoah*. As a starting point I recommend Lanzmann's own essays and interviews, which constitute both a commentary upon the film and a provocative critique of representation.[21] However, students are also alerted to the problems inherent in what Dominick LaCapra describes as the "prevalent critical practice of using [Lanzmann's views] to initiate, substantiate, or illustrate the critic's own conception of the film without subjecting them to critical scrutiny."[22] Felman's and Wajcman's influential essays on the film are read and discussed in conjunction with the more contestatory interpretations offered by Marianne Hirsch, Leo Spitzer, Tzvetan Todorov, and LaCapra.[23] Of particular interest in the context of ongoing debates about representability are recent readings by Michael Rothberg and Gary Weissman, who draw attention to aspects of Lanzmann's montage, *mise-en-scène* and camerawork which undermine an understanding of the film as straightforwardly anti-representational.[24] An attentive reviewing of *Shoah*'s exploration of processes of erasure, staging, reenactment, incarnation, and mimesis enables students to reconceptualize the refusal of representation often understood as the film's foundational ethical principle as possibly more ambivalent and conflicted than either Lanzmann's own pronouncements or some of his critics' condemnations allow.

This essay has suggested some ways in which *Shoah* and *Nuit et brouillard* can serve to deepen and enrich students' understanding of the relationships between history, testimony, and images, particularly in the light of mounting scepticism about the legitimacy of interdictions on representation. Enquiry along such lines necessarily prompts questions about the contemporary relevance and resonance of Lanzmann's and Resnais's particular aesthetic and ethical choices. Concerns about the evolving role of cinema in ongoing processes of commemoration, testimony, and mourning are acquiring fresh urgency with the advent of new and competing technologies of visual representation. In seminars on the two films students frequently allude to television coverage of recent atrocities; a recurrent point of reference is the endlessly repeated footage of the collapse of the Twin Towers on 11 September 2001. Such contributions can provoke discussions about the potentialities of cinema as a site of resistance to the televisual spectacularization of reality, which lead productively back to the ethical questions that preoccupy Resnais and Lanzmann. At a time when ever more innovative forms of visual witness are emerging, *Nuit et brouillard* and *Shoah* remain vital and prescient attempts to affirm and redefine cinema's singular role and responsibilities as vector of memory and vehicle of testimony.

Notes

1. Shoshana Felman, "Education and Crisis, or the Vicissitudes of Teaching," in Felman and Dori Laub, *Testimony: Crises of Witnessing in Literature, Psychoanalysis, and History* (New York: Routledge, 1992), 1–56 (1).
2. Ibid., 7, 52, 53, 54, 55.
3. The course was originally designed by Jill Forbes and Sue Harris. Since taking it over I have significantly revised the sections on Holocaust representation.
4. Judith Doneson, "The Use of Film in Teaching About the Holocaust," in *The Holocaust in University Teaching*, ed. Gideon Shimoni (Oxford: Pergamon, 1991), 15–23 (20).
5. Terri Ginsberg, "Towards a Critical Pedagogy of Holocaust and Film," *Review of Education, Pedagogy, and Cultural Studies* 26, 1 (January–March 2004): 47–59 (47–48, 51).
6. Recommended reading includes selections from Gilles Deleuze, *L'Image-temps: cinéma 2* (Paris: Les Editions de Minuit, 1985), Cathy Caruth, "Literature and the Re-enactment of Memory," in *Unclaimed Experience: Trauma, Narrative, and History* (Johns Hopkins University Press, 1996), 25–56.
7. Slavoj Žižek, "Camp Comedy," *Sight and Sound* 10, 4 (April 2000): 26–9.
8. Recommended reading includes Michel Foucault, "Anti-rétro: entretien avec Michel Foucault," *Cahiers du cinéma* 251–2 (July–August 1974): 5–15, Henry Rousso, *Le Syndrome de Vichy* (Paris: Les Editions de Seuil, 1987) and Naomi Greene, "Battles for Memory: Vichy Revisited," in *Landscapes of Loss: The National Past in Postwar French Cinema* (Princeton, NJ; Chichester: Princeton University Press, 1999), 64–97.
9. Two significant exceptions are Leo Spitzer's essay "'You Wanted History, I Give You History': Claude Lanzmann's *Shoah*," in *Teaching the Representation of the Holocaust*, ed. Marianne Hirsch and Irene Kacandes (New York: Modern Language Association, 2004), 412–21, and the brief discussion of teaching *Shoah* in Jean-François Forges, *Éduquer contre Auschwitz: histoire et mémoire* (Paris: ESF, 1997), 111–13.
10. Gillian Rose, *Mourning Becomes the Law: Philosophy and Representation* (Cambridge: Cambridge University Press, 1996), 41–43; Giorgio Agamben, *Remnants of Auschwitz*, trans. by Daniel Heller-Roazen (New York: Zone, 1999), 31–33; Jacques Rancière, "S'il y a de l'irreprésentable," in *L'Art et la mémoire des camps: représenter exterminer*, ed. Jean-Luc Nancy (Paris: Les Editions de Seuil, 2001), 81–102; Georges Didi-Huberman, "Images malgré tout," in *Mémoire des camps: photographies des camps de concentration et d'extermination nazies (1933–1999)*, ed. Clément Chéroux (Paris: Marval, 2001), 219–241 (230–1); Jean-Luc Nancy, *Au fond des images* (Paris: Les Editions de Galilée, 2003), 57–99.
11. Claude Lanzmann, "Le Lieu et la parole," in Bernard Cuau and others, *Au sujet de Shoah, le film de Claude Lanzmann* (Paris: Belin, 1990), 293–305 (297).
12. Georges Didi-Huberman, *Images malgré tout* (Paris: Les Editions de Minuit, 2003); Gérard Wajcman, "De la croyance photographique," *Temps modernes* 613 (March–May 2001): 47–83.

13. Copies of the films are available in the college library for subsequent viewings.
14. Leo Bersani and Ulysse Dutoit, *Arts of Impoverishment: Beckett, Rothko, Resnais* (Cambridge, MA: Harvard University Press, 1993), 187.
15. *Probing the Limits of Representation: Nazism and the "Final Solution,"* ed. by Saul Friedländer (Cambridge, MA: Harvard University Press, 1992); Berel Lang, *Holocaust Representation: Art within the Limits of History and Ethics* (Baltimore: Johns Hopkins University Press, 2000); Charles Krantz, "Teaching *Night and Fog*: History and Historiography," *Film and History* 15, 1 (February 1985): 2–15. Also useful in this context are the additional resources on the recently-released Arte DVD of *Nuit et brouillard*: a radio programme, "Nuit et brouillard, 1954–1994," produced for France Culture, which includes interviews with Resnais and Lanzmann, and a booklet of documentation pertaining to the film.
16. Didi-Huberman, *Images malgré tout;* Joshua Hirsch, *Afterimage: Film, Trauma and the Holocaust* (Philadelphia: Temple University Press, 2004); Emma Wilson, "Material Remains: *Night and Fog*," October 112, 1 (Spring 2005): 89–110.
17. Wilson, "Material Remains: *Night and Fog*," 109; Hirsch, *Afterimage*, 52; Vincent Lowy, *L'Histoire infilmable: les camps d'extermination nazis à l'écran* (Paris: L'Harmattan, 2001), 187.
18. The United States version of the New Yorker four-disc DVD set of *Shoah* includes a menu listing witnesses in the order they appear in the film and briefly summarizing their testimonies, allowing viewers to locate and access specific sequences with relative speed and ease.
19. Lanzmann, "Le Lieu et la parole," 295.
20. See in particular Claude Lanzmann, "Holocauste, la représentation impossible," *Le Monde* (Supplément Arts–Spectacles), 3 March 1994, i, vii.
21. Some key texts are collected in Bernard Cuau and others, *Au sujet de Shoah, le film de Claude Lanzmann* (Paris: Belin, 1990).
22. Dominick LaCapra, "Lanzmann's *Shoah*: 'Here There Is No Why'," in *History and Memory after Auschwitz* (Ithaca: Cornell University Press, 1998), 95–138 (97).
23. Shoshana Felman, "The Return of the Voice: Claude Lanzmann's *Shoah*," in Felman and Dori Laub, *Testimony: Crises of Witnessing in Literature, Psychoanalysis, and History* (New York: Routledge, 1992), 204–83; Gérard Wajcman, *L'Objet du siècle* (Lagrasse: Verdier, 1998); Marianne Hirsch and Leo Spitzer, "Gendered Translations: Claude Lanzmann's *Shoah*," in *Gendering War Talk*, ed. Miriam Cooke and Angela Woollacott (Princeton, NJ: Princeton University Press, 1993), 3–19; Tzvetan Todorov, *Face à l'extrême* (Paris: Les Editions de Seuil, 1991), 248–55.
24. Michael Rothberg, *Traumatic Realism: the Demands of Holocaust Representation* (Minneapolis: Minnesota University Press, 2000), 231–44; Gary Weissman, *Fantasies of Witnessing: Postwar Efforts to Experience the Holocaust* (Ithaca; London: Cornell University Press, 2004), 189–206.

9
Teaching Primo Levi
Rachel Falconer

How and why might one choose to teach Holocaust literature in the context of other topics generally studied in the course of an English literature degree, such as the examination of a particular literary tradition, historical period, or theoretical approach? Does the inclusion of Holocaust testimony amongst predominantly fictional or imaginative texts weaken the impact of the testimony? Is the work of testimony dehistoricized or elevated to an iconic or mythic status as a result of being read in a literary context? Conversely, what advantages might be gained by studying testimony alongside literary fiction? To explore these questions, I would like to focus on my experience of teaching Primo Levi's *If This is a Man*, as part of a third year, elective, undergraduate module about descents into the underworld, from Dante's *Inferno* to contemporary film (*Apocalypse Now*), fiction (Alasdair Gray's *Lanark* and other novels) and poetry (Peter Reading's *Perduta Gente* and Alice Notley's *The Descent of Alette*).[1] The module has evolved slowly over the period of a decade or more, but it has now acquired a more or less permanent shape, with Levi at the centre of the reading syllabus.

The most obvious question raised by the inclusion of Levi in this "Literature of Descent" module is whether it justifiable or even advisable to study Holocaust testimony in the context of literary fiction. In my view, there are compelling reasons for doing so. First, it exposes material to students who might otherwise be reluctant (for a variety of reasons) to take on the subject. Secondly, it counteracts the tendency towards ghettoization of literature about the Holocaust. Thirdly, it reflects my own introduction to the literature of the Holocaust, which equally applies to many students on an English literature degree course. That is to say, I came to Primo Levi with some knowledge of imaginative literature about Hell and underworlds, and a preexisting interpretive framework for descent narratives. And finally, when interspersed with other texts, Holocaust literature can offset the effects of "teacher trauma", not to mention the possibly traumatizing effects on students who may be encountering such material for the first time.

But there are also interesting, more specific questions raised by the "Descent" module at Sheffield. The *katabatic* (Greek term, meaning "going down") literature studied in this module traditionally traces the breakdown of a protagonist's psyche, a confrontation with Otherness, and a return journey of some kind.[2] The *narration* of the journey, moreover, constitutes another "descent to the underworld," in the sense that the "survivor" of the actual journey returns to Hell through memory in search of something lost, some otherworldly wisdom or knowledge, or some elusive understanding of present identity. Primo Levi's *If This is a Man* is read in Week Six, just before our mid-term break for Reading Week (see Appendix for the syllabus of weekly reading). In this position, Levi's text provides a pivotal point and a bridge between pre- and post-1945 descent narratives.

Specialists in Holocaust literature will be, no doubt, immediately wary of a narrative tradition that represents a hero returning from the experience of mythic horror, bearing wisdom and an otherworldly authority to relate the experience without challenge from a non-survivor. If so, they will have anticipated the function of Levi's text, placed midway in the reading syllabus, which is precisely to disrupt the inherited cultural, religious and literary assumptions of this narrative tradition. I have chosen to position Levi at the dead centre of the module, so that the students' experience of reading *If This is a Man* will be felt as a disruption to a different kind of academic study. It is, notably, the only work of non-fiction on the module, not to mention the only example of Holocaust testimony. In such a context, reading *If This is a Man* will always come as a shock. There is always a marked change of atmosphere from this point in the module onwards, as students fresh from reading Virgil, Dante, Milton, and Blake, switch gear and begin to think of Hell as a tangibly real, historically specific condition.[3]

In this way, I hope to reproduce at the level of pedagogy the experience Levi describes, on his return to Italy after the war:

> As the train, more tired than us, climbed toward the Italian frontier it snapped in two like an overtaut cable . . . we knew that on the thresholds of our homes, for good or ill, a trial awaited us, and we anticipated it with fear. We felt in our veins the poison of Auschwitz, flowing together with our thin blood . . . We felt the weight of centuries on our shoulders, we felt oppressed by a year of ferocious memories . . . With these thoughts, which kept us from sleep, we passed our first night in Italy, as the train slowly descended the deserted, dark Adige Valley. (Levi 1995: 378)

Here as elsewhere Levi refers to a caesural break between his pre- and post-Auschwitz lives. Some might argue that my intention to stage a sense of shock in the students constitutes questionably manipulative pedagogic practice.

In answer to this objection, I would argue, firstly, that some techniques must be developed to counteract the desensitization of students who may have been overexposed to a limited range of images from the Holocaust. Secondly, the shock is well ballasted by less controversial material on both sides of the week we spend with Levi. Indeed the ordering of texts may also work in the opposite direction (against shock), demonstrating that Holocaust testimony emerges from an imaginative tradition which interrogates the nature of identity in conditions of extreme physical and psychological breakdown. As a study like Todorov's *Facing the Extreme* demonstrates, Holocaust testimony challenges and redefines our understanding of subjectivity in relation to the limits of human experience;[4] so too does *katabatic* literature. Death, torture, and criminality are the extremes which the subject endures, and by which subjectivity is measured, in this ancient literary tradition. *If This is a Man* is a particularly apt text to illustrate the intertextuality of some Holocaust testimony, because Levi consciously relates his experience in the *lager* to earlier, literary representations of underworld journeys, notably Dante's *Inferno*, Coleridge's "The Ancient Mariner," Conrad's *Heart of Darkness* and Eliot's *The Waste Land*.[5]

My third response to the objection anticipated above, would be that juxtaposing and ordering texts in such a way as to allow them to inter-illuminate each other in unforeseen ways is characteristic of Levi's own practice as a writer. This is especially true of his late work, *The Search for Roots*, in which he indirectly narrates a kind of autobiography by providing a series of extracts from his favourite books.[6] A map at the end of the Preface suggests alternative routes through the extracts that a reader might take, each route or pathway with its dominant theme: "man suffers unjustly" or, conversely, "the dignity of man" (Levi 2001: 8–9).

Thus, in Week Six, using *If This is a Man* as a springboard, we discuss how survivors of atrocity represent the experience to readers and themselves, in ways that are embedded in existing narrative traditions. We explore ways in which, when survivors talk and write about having "been through Hell," they consciously or unconsciously draw on a wealth of inherited ideas and images about Hell. This inheritance derives not only from literary and religious discourses but also psychoanalytic and economic ones.[7] With the idea of Hell comes a fixed cast of characters (Satan, Minos, Charon, and others) and still more importantly, an anticipated narrative trajectory of descent, inversion, and return. Once again, Levi's *If This is a Man* is an apt text with which to frame this discussion because he is intensely aware of this cultural inheritance. He both plays against this tradition ironically, and deploys it seriously. Though one may argue about whether to describe Levi as an Enlightenment or post-Enlightenment writer, in my view he belongs to the history of *katabatic* literature, which, significantly, is known to classical scholars as the "wisdom tradition."[8] In the Afterword to *If This is a Man*, Levi notes, "a friend of mine . . . says that the camp was her university. I think I can say the same thing" (Levi 1995: 398).[9] Levi's belief that writing about the Holocaust *can* communicate meaning, that it is something from which we can positively learn, is in itself a justification for the inclusion of Holocaust testimony on a literature degree course.

Certainly, there are drawbacks in choosing just one text to bear this weight of signification, especially a text so often canonized as Levi's *If This is a Man*. If it seems over-familiar to specialists, however, it is rarely so to undergraduates; and one might recall that as few as sixty years ago, Levi had practically no willing readers. On the question of canonization, I would say simply that I have not selected *If This is a Man* because it is canonical (although it may be one reason the text chose me); I teach it because of its intrinsic merits and because of its conscious intertextuality. As many critics have noted, there is a rich and complex dialogue with Dante in *If This is a Man*.[10] But there are also more general ideas about Holocaust testimony that are thrown into sharp relief when studied alongside imaginary journeys into Hell. Here I will briefly outline six specific issues we address in our seminar discussions, which students are then free to explore in their written assessments. The module is assessed by two essays (1500 and 2500 words) or by one essay of 4000 words (the student is asked to declare a preference for one of these options by Week Three of the module).

First (though not necessarily in this order) we explore questions about the representation of narrative time in testimony. Following the seminar discussion, one student wrote on *If This is a Man*, "whilst there is some attempt at seeking coherence, the narrator as a whole does not resist the impact of trauma." The student analysed the sequencing of tenses to support this argument, quoting in particular the passage describing the deportee's entry into the camp: "Then the lorry stopped, and we saw a large door . . . We climb down" (Levi 1995: 28). Against such lapses into a traumatized present tense, the student compared the use of chronological and diary-time at the end of the text, as well as the sense of seasonal change in the camp that the text as a whole so vividly conveys.

Secondly, we examine the use of shifting narratorial perspectives in *If This is a Man*. We discuss problems and tensions involved in the narrator's representation of other prisoners in the camp, problems which are thrown into relief by the comparison with Dante. In *Inferno*, as in many classical underworld narratives, the protagonist travels through Hell as an observer not an inhabitant, and he remains magically exempt from punishment. There are connections here to be explored in Holocaust testimony, concerning a narrator's necessary surplus of knowledge, and the obvious fact that the narrator has survived and escaped, while many of those s/he describes may not have. Contrasts can be pursued here between the poet Dante's emergent sense of retributive justice, and the "survivor guilt" felt by many former concentration camp prisoners. We also discuss the split in perspective between Levi as present narrator and as past *häftling*. The horizon of expectation of descent narratives (as well as autobiography, conversion narratives, and many forms of *bildungsroman*) includes a divide between past, imperfect and present, perfected or completed self; in part the *raison d'être* of such narratives is to explain and justify how the present self came to be. In descent, and religious conversion, narratives, the built-in before-and-after structure is still more sharply delineated.[11] The wayfaring pilgrim (in Dante, or Bunyan for example) journeys through Hell in a state of sin. At the journey's end, the pilgrim has become the poet (the two terms used traditionally in Dante scholarship to distinguish character from narrator); he has achieved grace, become the Pauline new man, *and* acquired the infallible authority to relate the story. Levi's testimony challenges this generic expectation (with, one might add, its Christian arc of sin and salvation) by presenting *two* later selves, on the one hand, the camp *vecchio* or old-timer, who has survived a year at camp and acquired a wealth of infernal wisdom, and on the other hand, the narrator who, on many levels, wishes to divest himself of this knowledge.[12] He knows himself to be "saved" yet views this Dantean category with profound suspicion.

Thirdly, we discuss questions of tone, style, and narrative structure. Many Holocaust testimonies, including Levi's, are narrated in a flat, pared-down, anti-aesthetic style. The contrast with pre-modern descent narratives could not be more striking or extreme. Pre-modern Judeo-Christian writers are in general much freer in their descriptions of Hell than of Heaven, about which there are many more theological prescriptions; hence underworld journeys tended to be narrated in baroque style or a melodramatic, hyperbolic tone.[13] Interestingly, many students take exception to Levi's dispassionate tone, declaring they would "trust" him more if he showed emotion more overtly and if he were more explicitly judgemental toward his captors. We then go on to discuss how testimonial narratives produce a sense of authenticity and, or as opposed to, reliability and objectivity.

From this, it is a short step to discussing the representation of memory in *If This is a Man*. Beginning with the poem which precedes the narrative ("Consider if this is a man"), we move on to focus on two episodes in particular: Levi's trial before Dr Pannwitz (Chapter 10), and the journey to the soup-queue with Pikkolo, in which Levi remembers Dante's *Canto of Ulysses* (Dante, *Inferno* 26; Levi 1995, Chapter 11). The first of these episodes conveys Levi's horrified sense of complicity with the SS chemist as they discover a shared body of knowledge. The second explores both the power of memory to restore identity, and the destructive potential of memories that cannot be passed on.

A fifth topic—an unescapable one, is the contrasting representation of evil and Otherness in Holocaust testimony such as Levi's.[14] Here again, there is a stark contrast with earlier representations of Satan, whether complex and psychologically rounded (Milton's) or anti-climactically, flatly allegorical (Dante's).[15] This leads to the final topic, Levi's specific intertextual dialogues with earlier *katabatic* narratives, especially Dante's *Inferno*. Some of the points of connection that students regularly find between Dante and Levi include: Dante's description of Charon the ferryman and Levi's description of the German truckdriver who delivers them to Auschwitz; Dante's Minos, judging the souls of the dead, and Levi's representation of the *selekcja* of October 1944; the infernal repetition of labour and punishment and the sense of eternal suffering conveyed in both texts; again in both texts, the sense of leaving historical time and entering the realm of myth; the sense of Hell/Auschwitz as a space in which identity is lost or unmade. Conversely, students also discover useful contrasts between Dante and Levi. In seminar discussions, and in assessed work, students point out, for example: the eloquence of the damned in *Inferno* and the stature they acquire when recounting their histories, as opposed to the severely degraded language of the *lager* prisoners; Dante's Hell as an expression of divine *Justizia*, and Hell governed by the principle of *contrapasso* (punishment suited to the crime) in contrast to Auschwitz, in which there is no rationale for punishment (*"hier ist kein warum"* (Levi 1995: 35)); the serious trial of the soul in *Inferno*, as opposed to the demonic trial of the prisoners, trial as farce, in *If This is a Man* (although in another sense, the prisoners can choose to see their experience as a kind of trial of the soul as well).

Reading and then writing about Primo Levi tends to destabilize many of the students' notions about literary genres. It also raises technically interesting questions about the way narrative works, questions relating to intertextuality, narratorial perspective, and narrative temporality. And it demonstrates the complex interrelation between historical accuracy and imaginative invention in Holocaust testimony. But it is also illuminating to recall the common mistakes and misconceptions that recur in student essays, because these may suggest some of the limitations of the module as it currently stands.

Many students refer to Levi's *If This is a Man* as a novel, and the name Auschwitz is frequently spelled incorrectly; such basic errors are symptomatic of a historical ignorance, which in part comes from teaching the Holocaust in the context of literary fiction. Following from the examples of descent heroes Odysseus, Aeneas, and Dante, students sometimes place a mistaken emphasis on Levi's heroic survival (so too, does the title of the American edition, *Survival in Auschwitz*). Likewise, they may try to locate a satanic character in the text (such Dr Pannwitz, or the evil Kapo) whereas I think that to look for a single, human source of evil is to misread the text. (Or perhaps, if there is a Dantean Satan in *If This is a Man*, it is the *sonderkommando* whose public hanging is described in "The Last One"—in other words, a victim who also contributed to administering the final punishment of other prisoners. Again, an interesting contrast emerges, as Levi's "last one" revolts and therefore (in Levi's eyes) dies a hero's death.) Students also sometimes assume (as I do myself) that Levi writes from a position of unquestionable authority, like Dante the poet. But this fails to take into account Levi's own ambivalence about his "saved" status, as both Holocaust survivor and writer.

One might also address the question of what happens on the module after students have read *If This is a Man*. In returning to fictional narratives, am I not counter-acting the disruptive effect I have deliberately staged earlier, implicitly suggesting that in post-1945 *katabatic* literature, it is back to business as normal, as if the Holocaust had not permanently destabilized our concept of the underworld? In one sense, however, this is precisely the point: post-Holocaust, narratives about psychological descents to Hell do not cease to be written. But as I hope the latter half of my module demonstrates, all of these contemporary fictional narratives represent infernal journeys in ways that have been profoundly influenced by Holocaust survivor testimony. For example, although they are works of fiction, they all represent Hell as an actual, material, historically realized place or event.[16] And, reflecting our Holocaust inheritance, in all these contemporary texts, the protagonist does not descend to Hell, because he or she is already there, *sul fundo*, at the start of the text. The question for later writers is not how to descend to, and return from, Hell, but how to acquire a kind of double vision, an ability to stand both within and outside the experience of historical atrocity.

The strongest reason for teaching Levi's *If This is a Man* in the context of a literature module is that students often become deeply engaged with Levi's writing and ideas after even this briefest of encounters. And this engagement leads them to pursue their study of the Holocaust elsewhere on the degree course, in other undergraduate modules, in dissertation topics, and in modules and dissertations at MA level. So while I have described the effect of reading *If This is a Man* as a caesura running through the middle of the course, I would also see it functioning as a bridge to further study. As so often happens with Primo Levi, just when one appears to be nearing a conclusion, he provokes a lateral shift in thinking, and a fresh engagement with Holocaust literature in a new context.

Appendix

University of Sheffield   Session 2006–07
Department of English Literature   Autumn Semester

Lit 367: Literature of Descent
Dr Rachel Falconer

Reading Schedule

Descent narratives, classical to modern

Week 1:
Introductions, Virgil, *Aeneid* Book 6 and other classical descent journeys
Reading from course pack: (1) Literature of Descent: a brief introduction (by RF) and (2) Atwood, Margaret, *Negotiating with the Dead, a Writer on Writing*: 137–61.

Week 2:
Dante, *Inferno* Cantos 1–17
Narrative structures and motifs of descent literature
Reading from course pack: Clark, Raymond, *Catabasis: Vergil and the Wisdom Tradition*: 13–36.

Week 3:
Dante, *Inferno* Cantos 18–34
Reading from course pack: Auerbach, Erich, *Mimesis*: 151–76.

Week 4:
Milton, *Paradise Lost* Books 1–2 (*Norton Anthology*)
William Blake, *The Marriage of Heaven and Hell* (*Norton Anthology*).

Week 5:
T. S. Eliot, *The Waste Land* and Joseph Conrad, *Heart of Darkness*; reading from course pack: Hillman, James, *The Dream and the Underworld*: 23–32; Pike, David, *Passage through Hell: Modernist Descents, Medieval Underworlds*: 1–34.

Post-1945 descent narratives

Week 6:
Primo Levi, *If This is a Man*
Reading from course pack: Steiner, George, *Bluebeard's Castle: Some Notes Towards the Re-definition of Culture*: 31–48.

Week 7:
Reading week, no seminar; course pack: Descent Narrative in Theory (RF).

Week 8:
Film: Francis Ford Coppola, dir., *Apocalypse Now*.

Week 9:
Fiction (1): Alasdair Gray, *Lanark*.

Week 10:
Fiction (2): Angela Carter, *The Passion of New Eve*.

Week 11:
Poetry: Peter Reading, *Perduta Gente*; Alice Notley, *The Descent of Alette*.

Week 12:
Fiction (3): Salman Rushdie, *The Ground Beneath Her Feet*.

Notes

1. Primo Levi, *If This is a Man* and *The Truce*, tr. Stuart Woolf (London: Abacus, 1995); Francis Ford Coppola, dir., *Apocalypse Now* (Zoetrope Studios, 1979); Alasdair Gray, *Lanark: a Life in Four Books* (London: Pan Books, 1994); Salman Rushdie, *The Ground Beneath Her Feet* (London: Jonathan Cape, 1999); Angela Carter, *The Passion of New Eve* (London: Virago, 1982); Peter Reading, "Perduta Gente", *Collected Poems 2: Poems 1985–1996* (Glasgow: Bloodaxe, 1996): 159–215; Alice Notley, *The Descent of Alette* (London: Penguin, 1992).

2. Margaret Atwood provides a lively introduction to descent journey narratives in *Negotiating with the Dead, a Writer on Writing* (London: Virago, 2003). Much drier, though more comprehensive and scholarly is Raymond Clark's *Catabasis: Vergil and the Wisdom Tradition* (Amsterdam: B. R. Gruner, 1979).
3. Virgil, *Virgil*, tr. H. Rushton Fairclough (London: William Heinemann Ltd., 1978). Vol 1: *Eclogues, Georgics, Aeneid 1–6*. Vol 2: *Aeneid 7–12*, minor poems; Dante Alighieri, *The Divine Comedy*, tr. Charles Singleton (Princeton, NJ: Princeton University Press, 1989), 6 vols; John Milton, *Milton: Paradise Lost*, ed. A. Fowler (Harlow: Longman, 1998, 2nd edition); William Blake, *The Marriage of Heaven and Hell* (Oxford: Oxford University Press, 1975). There are, of course, many ways to read these pre-modern Hells as fully political and historical. For such an approach to Dante, see Erich Auerbach's now classic essay, "Farinata and Cavalcante" in *Mimesis*, tr. Willard Trask (New York: Doubleday Anchor Books, 1957): 151–76.
4. Tzvetan Todorov, *Facing the Extreme: Moral Life in the Concentration Camps* (London: Weidenfeld and Nicolson, 1999).
5. Samuel Taylor Coleridge, "The Rime of the Ancient Mariner", in *Coleridge: Poems and Prose selected by Kathleen Raine*, London: Penguin, 1985): 37–55; Joseph Conrad, *Heart of Darkness*, ed. R. Kimbrough (London: Norton, 1988); T. S. Eliot, *The Waste Land, and other Poems*, introduced by Vasant Shane (London: Faber, 1971).
6. Primo Levi, *The Search for Roots*, tr. Peter Forbes (London: Allen Lane, Penguin, 2001).
7. For an overview of this inheritance, see Rachel Falconer, "Introduction", *Hell in Contemporary Literature: Western Descent Narratives since 1945* (Edinburgh: Edinburgh University Press, 2005); Rosalind Williams, *Notes on the Underground: an Essay on Technology, Society, and the Imagination* (Cambridge, MA: MIT Press, 1992); David Pike, *Passage Through Hell: Modernist Descents, Medieval Underworlds* (London: Cornell University Press, 1997). For a Jungian approach to classical underworld myths, see James Hillman, *The Dream and the Underworld* (New York: Harper and Row, 1979).
8. See Raymond Clark, *Catabasis: Vergil and the Wisdom Tradition* (Amsterdam: B. R. Gruner, 1979). An Enlightenment writer in the sense that he values rationality, objectivity and transparency in narrative, Levi is nevertheless singularly Romantic in his interpretations of the Book of Job, *The Odyssey*, Dante's *Inferno*, and Coleridge's "The Ancient Mariner" (to name but a few texts); see the head notes to his extracts from these texts in *The Search for Roots*.
9. See also Primo Levi, *The Drowned and the Saved*, tr. Raymond Rosenthal (London: Abacus, 1989): 114; and Ferdinando Camon, *Conversations with Primo Levi*, tr. John Shepley (Marlboro, VT: the Marlboro Press, 1989).
10. See L. M. Gunzberg, "Down Among the Dead Men: Levi and Dante in Hell", *Modern Language Studies* 16, 1 (Winter 1986): 10–28; Zvi Jagendorf, "Primo Levi Goes for Soup and Remembers Dante," *Raritan* 12, 4 (Spring 1993): 31–51; Mirna Cicioni, *Primo Levi: Bridges of Knowledge*

(Oxford: Berg, 1995); Nicholas Patruno, *Understanding Primo Levi* (South Carolina: University of South Carolina Press, 1995); Anthony Rudolf, *At an Uncertain Hour: Primo Levi's War Against Oblivion* (London: the Menard Press, 1990); and Judith Woolf, *The Memory of the Offence: Primo Levi's If This is a Man* (Leicester: University Texts, 1995), especially Chapter 5, "A New Inferno": 51–64.

11. On the dynamics of conversion narrative, see John Freccero, *The Poetics of Conversion*, ed. Rachel Jacoff (Cambridge, MA: Harvard University Press, 1986).
12. I have discussed this triangulation of perspectives in *Hell in Contemporary Literature*, Chapter 3.
13. See Carol Zaleski, *Otherworld Journeys: Accounts of Near-Death Experience in Medieval and Modern Times* (Oxford: Oxford University Press, 1987).
14. Interested students are also referred to Susan Neiman's useful study, *Evil in Modern Thought* (Princeton, NJ: Princeton University Press, 2002).
15. See Milton, *Paradise Lost* Books 1–2, and Dante, *Inferno*, Canto 33.
16. On the materialization of Hell in history, I refer students to George Steiner's *In Bluebeard's Castle: Some Notes Towards the Re-definition of Culture* (London: Faber, 1971).

10
Teaching Holocaust Literature and Film to History Students: Teaching *The Pawnbroker* (1961/1965)

Tim Cole

In this essay, I explore the ways that I use Holocaust literature and film when teaching history students, through a case study of my classroom use of Edward Lewis Wallant's 1961 novel, *The Pawnbroker*, which formed the basis for Sidney Lumet's 1965 film of the same name. Wallant's novel and Lumet's film feature in my teaching of the history of representation of the Holocaust in the post-war world alongside other films—Claude Lanzmann's *Shoah* (1985) and Roberto Benigni's *Life is Beautiful* (1998)—Art Spiegelman's *Maus* (1986 & 1991), Binjamin Wilkomirski's *Fragments* (1996), as well as a host of other post-war representations including memorials, museums, fine art, historical texts, and Holocaust trials.

Given the plethora of Holocaust novels and films available, I should, perhaps, begin by briefly discussing my choice of *The Pawnbroker* as one of the texts that I use in the classroom. As with the other films that I teach, there is a dual motivation for my choice. On the one hand, *The Pawnbroker* features in my teaching for rather stereotypically historian's reasons: the time and place of both the novel and film's production and initial reception. The attraction of this particular novel and film is that both are a product of 1960s America, and specifically those years between what have been seen as two defining events in the rising awareness of the Holocaust in

Jewish-American consciousness: the Eichmann Trial (1961) and the Six-Day War (1967).[1] On the other hand, *The Pawnbroker* is also important in raising a number of broader themes central to debates over Holocaust representation, in particular the "universalization" of the Holocaust and the use of Christian redemptive imagery in telling Holocaust stories. These two underlying motivations—the time and place of production and the broader themes raised by the text—can also be seen behind my choice of *Shoah* and *Life is Beautiful* as films for classroom discussion in the weeks following our analysis of *The Pawnbroker*. *Shoah* provides opportunities for discussion of the representation and reception of the Holocaust in the 1980s, as well as accessing broader debates over Polish responses to Holocaust representation, historical reconstruction in Holocaust film, and the relationship between the film-maker, historian, and survivor in narrating this past. *Life is Beautiful* shifts the timescale into the 1990s, with a focus upon both the production of the film in 1990s Italy, and its international reception. It also raises important issues about the use of humour in telling Holocaust stories, a subject central to Terrence Des Pres's important essay on "Holocaust Laughter."[2]

In broader terms then, my teaching of Holocaust literature and film to history students tends to be dominated by two main concerns, which can perhaps best be dubbed the historical and the theoretical. As a historian, chronology matters to me, and so my initial focus is upon the historical context within which any literary or filmic text was produced and initially received. In short, I am concerned with viewing Holocaust texts as the products of a particular time and place, rather than primarily as part of the output of a particular author or director. But, I am also interested in encouraging students to grapple with broader theoretical (and aesthetical and ethical) questions about Holocaust representation—what Saul Friedlander memorably dubbed "the limits of representation" of this particular event.[3] Indeed it is here that I find the greatest classroom debate is generated. My hope is that discussion of how the Holocaust has been represented encourages a degree of self-reflection on the part of my students, such that thinking is not only on how the disciplinary "Other"—not the historian, but the filmmaker or novelist—has represented this past, but also how we as historians choose to narrate the Holocaust. This is something that I wish to return to at the close of this essay, but before doing so, I will explore a little more fully how I use *The Pawnbroker* to raise a number of historical and theoretical issues with students of the history of Holocaust representation.

Historical approaches: *The Pawnbroker*, the Holocaust, Holocaust survivors and 1960s America

As I mentioned at the outset, one major attraction of Wallant's novel and Lumet's film is that both are products of 1960s America which is a period that Peter Novick has seen as "years of transition" as far as American Holocaust consciousness is concerned.[4] Surprisingly, Novick deals with neither the novel nor the film in the pages of his provocative history of the shifting representation of the Holocaust in post-war America. However, these texts are useful in exploring engagement with the Holocaust and more specifically a Holocaust survivor in 1960s America. They provide a cultural product to examine in addressing the emerging debate over when and why the Holocaust came to feature large in American life.[5] As they read the novel, watch the film, and read some of the contemporary press reviews of the film, I encourage students to keep historiographical debates over post-war silence about the Holocaust giving way increasingly to growing noise from the 1960s onwards in the back of their minds. Seeing *The Pawnbroker* as the product of a particular historical moment, I ask students to work with the text as evidence of the kinds of meanings given to the Holocaust—and specifically Holocaust survivors—in early to mid 1960s America.

One way into this is to ask students, as they read the novel and watch the film to think about how the tattooed numbers on Holocaust survivor Sol Nazerman's arm—an iconic Holocaust symbol in the contemporary world—are variously interpreted by the characters who encounter him. In the early part of the novel, there is a conversation between the survivor Sol Nazerman and his assistant in the pawn shop, Jesus Ortiz:

> "These here suits, Sol," he began, and then stared in puzzlement at the crudely tattooed numbers on his employer's thick, hairless arm. "Hey, what kind of tattoo you call that?" he asked.

"It's a secret society I belong to," Sol answered, with a scythelike curve to his mouth. "You could never belong. You have to be able to walk on the water."

"Okay, okay, mind my own business, hah," Ortiz said, his eyes still on the strange, codelike markings. How many secrets the big, pallid Jew has![6]

Jesus' puzzlement over the significance of these tattooed numbers continues through the novel. He is intrigued, indeed obsessed, with the significance of these tattooed numbers and the secrets that his employer possessed.[7] And it is clear that it was not only Jesus who struggled to interpret the mysterious tattoo:

> Through the hours, others besides Jesus Ortiz found time to wonder at the peculiar ragged numbers etched like false veins under the skin of his arm, or to speculate on the graven cast of his fleshy, spectacled face. But the Pawnbroker kept his secret, for while some of them might surmise some of the facts of his history, none of them could know its real truth. And as he plied his trade, each of them took away only a feeling of something quite huge and terrible.[8]

Whilst his assistant and customers remain bemused by these tattooed numbers, others realize their significance. For the well-meaning social worker Marilyn Birchfield, glimpsing the numbers suddenly explains why Sol Nazerman is the man he is:

> And then, just when he had her on the point of angrily humiliated departure, her eyes fell on the blue numbers on his arm. Her eyes went dreamy with pity, and she looked back up to his strange, ugly face with an exasperating humility, armoured now beyond his insult.
>
> "I am sorry, Mr Nazerman," she said. "You're right, and I apologise. Surprisingly, there are times when even I recognise my tactlessness. I guess I was irritated by your manner when I first came in, and I probably decided, half-consciously, to work you over."

"Why apologise? My manner had not changed for the better, has it?"

"Not really, I'm afraid," she said with a little laugh. "But now, somehow, it doesn't bother me anymore."[9]

Her desire to save Nazerman from his past is such that she dreams that this distinctive marking begins to fade:

> Later, she woke for a minute or two and stared at his gray face, all slack with sleep. She looked at the blue numbers on his arm and she became sad. But then she convinced herself that the numbers looked fainter, that they might disappear altogether in time. She dozed again.[10]

But it is not only Marilyn Birchfield who realizes the significance of these tattooed numbers. Also knowledgeable are another survivor collecting for the Jewish Appeal,[11] the African-American doctor who treats Tessie's dying father,[12] and the gang boss, who is money-laundering through Sol's pawn shop.[13]

Throughout the novel—and also the film—students identify that there are those for whom the tattooed numbers are shorthand for the Holocaust, and those for whom their meaning is oblique. For Sol's tattoo to work in this way, is suggestive that tattooed numbers had not yet emerged as emblematic symbols of the Holocaust. The lack of knowledge on the part of some characters in *The Pawnbroker* resonates with survivors' memories of explaining away their tattooed arms in 1950s America, but the instant recognition of the tattoo representing a Holocaust past on the part of others seems closer to the later emergence of these numbers as one of the iconic images of the Holocaust.[14] The end result would appear to be support for Novick's sense of the 1960s as "years of transition" in American knowledge of the Holocaust.

The ambiguous meaning given to the numbers tattooed on Sol's arm can be read, I think, as signalling that the Holocaust itself was not the iconic event in 1960s America that it was to become in the early 1990s.[15] Certainly this sense of the relative marginality of the Holocaust as a theme within 1960s American culture, is borne out when looking at the reception of the film. As Leonard Leff has demonstrated in his uncovering of the history of turning this novel into a film, eyebrows were raised over the film's subject matter.[16]

Once released, *New York Times* critic Bosley Crowther, expressed his sense of the novelty of "this most uncommon film, which projects a disagreeable subject with power and cogency."[17] Giving students the chance to work with reviews of the film in the press in 1965, allows them to attempt to use their historical imagination to grasp something of the initial reactions to this film: reactions which often surprise them, given their own very different time and place, and also their exposure to the last few decades of scholarship on Holocaust representation.

Exposure to the scholarship on survivors, as well as survivors' own writings, means that one of the things that is particularly surprising for students when they read and view *The Pawnbroker* is the way in which the Holocaust survivor Sol Nazerman is represented. On the opening page of the novel, students encounter him for the first time, walking through a snow-covered New York at 7.30 in the morning:

> Crunch, crunch, crunch.
> It could almost have been the pleasant sound of someone walking over clean white snow. But the sight of the great, bulky figure, with its puffy face, its heedless dark eyes distorted behind the thick lenses of strangely old-fashioned glasses, dispelled any thought of pleasure.[18]

From the outset, it is clear that Sol Nazerman is no ordinary man, and indeed it appears he—or rather it—is not truly human.[19] Throughout both novel and film, the overwhelming image of Nazerman is of someone who has been damaged by his traumatic past, and rendered incapable of "normal" human emotions and relationships. Nowhere is this more apparent than in the scenes where Sol interacts with Tessie, the widow of his friend, with whom he has loveless sex. When her father dies, he is unable to mourn with her. Sol Nazerman is shown as essentially dysfunctional, someone who is unable to mourn yet alone love. He is a bitter and amoral—if not immoral—man who abuses because he was abused.

This dysfunctional "displaced European Jew" as critic Bosley Crowther described Nazerman, is

> . . . a man who has reasonably eschewed a role of involvement and compassion in a brutal and bitter world and has found his life

barren and rootless as a consequence . . . To view this remarkable picture . . . as merely a mordant melodrama of a displaced European Jew who runs a pawnshop in New York's Harlem and is caught up in some evil doings there is to miss the profound dilemma and melancholy of its central character and the broader significance of his detachment and inability to adjust.

This man, played by Mr Steiger with a mounting intensity that carries from a state of listless ennui to a point of passion where it seems he's bound to burst, has good enough reason for detachment. He has been through the horror of the concentration camps, has lost his immediate family, has seen his best friend tortured and killed. This terrible traumatic experience has left him intellectually drained and emotionally numb. He has a fitful affair with his friend's widow but looks on people as "rejects, scum".[20]

The image of Nazerman developed in the novel and film is quite at odds with later notions of the survivor that emerged in the 1980s and 1990s, in particular around the person of Elie Wiesel. With Wiesel, survivors emerged as near celebrity figures with their unique experience of the Holocaust "kingdom" and the moral authority that this conveyed upon their voice. In setting the two images up against each other, I encourage students to draw upon the historiography on survivors, and in particular the important work of Henry Greenspan, who reminds us that,

> before survivors became "the survivors" they were known by other names. For many years . . . they were "the refugees", the "greeners", or simply "the ones who were there" . . . they evoked a shifting combination of pity, fear, revulsion, and guilt . . . to be singled out as a Holocaust survivor meant to be singled out indeed: a "sick and needy relative", "a specimen to be observed".[21]

That characterization of survivors as "sick" and dysfunctional is one that Greenspan sees continuing and being developed as the notion of "survival" and "survivors" became more important from the 1970s onwards. It became medicalized, he suggests, as a "psychiatric discourse." However it was joined by another very different—and I think increasingly dominant—discourse which he terms the "celebratory discourse." This is the discourse that celebrates survivors as "heroic witnesses, tellers of tales, redeemers of the human spirit and of hope,"[22] which is a discourse absent from *The Pawnbroker*. The character of Sol Nazermann raises critical questions about the ways in which Holocaust survivors have been perceived and represented, and how (and why) those images have changed. He provides a useful contrast for students to work with as they explore other representations (and self-representations) of Holocaust survivors.

Theoretical approaches: *The Pawnbroker*, compared history, christological symbolism, and doing history

Rooting *The Pawnbroker* very much in the time and place of its production and initial reception, is also central when I use the text to explore a range of what can perhaps be dubbed theoretical issues raised by the novel and film. As they read the novel and watch the film, I ask students to ask (as I do with all the texts we examine) how much the representations are about the Holocaust and how much about other things of relevance to contemporaries. There is nothing particularly novel about such an approach. It is the premise of Judith Doneson's *The Holocaust in American Film*, where she suggests that,

> American films that deal with the Holocaust serve a dual function. Yes, they focus on themes portraying National Socialism, and the persecution of the Jews; but they also explore contemporary issues that were and are germane to American society at the time of their appearance. Consequently, the analysis must proceed on both levels: on the salient level, the one that depicts the Holocaust itself, and on the latent level, the one that explains a particular film's contemporary meaning. The two are connected, of course. On the salient level, the Holocaust often works as a metaphor for the discourse taking place on the latent level. Thus the event—the Holocaust—is a function of its current environment as well as a reflection of its own history.[23]

In the case of *The Pawnbroker*, as many have pointed out, the Holocaust becomes a metaphor for—"compared history" as Doneson terms it[24]—contemporary issues relating to race. The context of early 1960s America and specifically civil rights (Civil Rights Act of 1964, summer riots of 1964, Voting Rights Act of 1965) informed not only production, but also reception of the film. Not only do the flashbacks in the film suggest an attempt on the part of Lumet to link events in 1960s Harlem with earlier Holocaust events (and thereby suggest at least some degree of continuity between American racism and the Holocaust) but it is clear that the initial reception of the film picked up on those linkages. For *New York Times* film critic Bosley Crowther, Lumet "has brilliantly intercut flashes of the horrors of the concentration camps with equally shocking visualizations of imprisonment in a free society. And he has clearly implied in terms of picture the irony of resemblances."[25] In a similar vein, Malcolm Boyd noted in *The Christian Century* how in the film, "the Nazi-Jewish holocaust is shown as openly related to the contemporary problems of the American Negro."[26]

That *The Pawnbroker* seems to be as much about 1960s America as the Holocaust and one of its survivors, raises important questions. Firstly, is there a sense in which other (perhaps all) Holocaust representations are about contemporary themes other than the Holocaust? Secondly, can *The Pawnbroker* be seen as early evidence of "Americanization" of the Holocaust, which uses this past to explore issues of relevance to America? Thirdly, how valid are the kinds of resemblances drawn in *The Pawnbroker*, and how appropriate is universalization of the Holocaust as a metaphor for other experiences of suffering?

These bigger questions about the nature and purpose of Holocaust representation are joined by another, which is particularly blatantly raised by *The Pawnbroker*. If not reading the novel and watching the film, then certainly in reading much of the secondary literature on *The Pawnbroker*, students cannot help but encounter the question of the appropriateness of Christian notions of redemption being applied to the Holocaust. A christological ending is particularly strong in the film, which closes with a scene of Sol plunging his hand into the pawn ticket spike and then leaving the shop with what many have interpreted as the stigmata. In the novel, there is no stigmata, but the narrative does have a clear-cut sense of (Christian) redemptive closure, which approaches a happy ending. It is after—and through—Jesus' death that Sol is shown as being able to grieve and maybe even love again. "All his anethetic numbness left him,"[27] and

> Then he began to cry . . . he realised he was crying for all his dead now, that all the dammed-up weeping had been released by

the loss of one irreplaceable Negro who had been his assistant and who had tried to kill him but who had ended by saving him . . .
. . . "Rest in peace, Ortiz, Mendel, Rubin, Ruth, Naomi, David . . . rest in peace," he said, still crying a little, but mostly for himself. He took a great breath of air, which seemed to fill parts of his lungs unused for a long time. And he took the pain of it, if not happily, like a martyr, at least willingly, like an heir. Then he began walking to the subway to take the long, underground journey to Tessie's house, to help her mourn.[28]

What I think is particularly interesting about the christological references, is that at the time they received nothing like the criticism that they have subsequently received.[29] So for example, the initial reviews on the whole do not condemn the film for the redemptive symbolism drawn from Christianity. For Bosley Crowther, the ending was clearly seen in Christian terms—"But it is not until he sees his young assistant—Jesus Ortiz is significantly his name—shot dead by holdup hoodlums during a courageous attempt to protect him that he senses the shame of his detachment. Then he slams his hand down on a paper spike to inflict upon himself the stigmata and acknowledge his burden of grief and guilt,"[30]—but this was not seen as problematic.

However, such sentiments could not be further from later academic criticism of the film, found for example in Ilan Avisar's damning of both the Christianization of Sol and the comparison drawn in the film between the Holocaust and Harlem.[31] Asking students to read Avisar's critique alongside contemporary receptions of the film which treated compared history and Christian symbolism as rather unproblematic, forces them to ask when and why such criticisms of Holocaust representation emerged, as well as what they make of such critiques. In many ways I don't want students to get too bogged down in debating the appropriateness or inappropriateness of the Christian imagery or the comparisons evoked in the novel and film themselves. My hope is that they move beyond what can become somewhat sterile debates to consider how and why "appropriateness" became central concerns to writers such as Avisar. His sentiments are part of a wider phenomenon observed by Hilene Flanzbaum, of cultural policing of "appropriate" and "inappropriate" Holocaust products in the 1980s and 1990s.[32] Flanzbaum raises important issues about the kinds of discourses—for example notions of "trivialization"—that are adopted in commenting on Holocaust literature and film. It encourages reflection on what questions we ask in our classroom discussion of (and writing on) Holocaust representations. In particular, what place if any (and my sense, contra Flanzbaum, is that sometimes there may be[33]) are there for raising the questions "how accurate is it?," "how appropriate is it?" and "does it trivialize the Holocaust?"

Grappling with questions about how to represent the Holocaust, as well as how to critique representations of the Holocaust leads, I hope, to increased self-reflection on the part of my students. As they study Holocaust literature and film, my desire is that students do not see Holocaust representation (and the host of theoretical, aesthetical and ethical questions raised by these representations) as simply something done by non-historians. Rather, I want history students to examine their own discipline's output and explore the historical writing on the Holocaust with which they are familiar, as another representation of this past. Looking again at the Holocaust historians they have read, my hope is that they ask questions about "compared history" (the *Historikerstreit* leaps to mind)[34] and the narrative strategies (including the use of "happy endings") adopted by Holocaust historians.[35] In short, I want to develop a degree of self-reflection upon what we do as historians with this past, and why.

One thing that I find immensely productive in teaching film and literature to historians, is the exposure to a varied secondary literature that teaching something like *The Pawnbroker* opens students up to. The advantage of a multi-disciplinary reading list is not simply that it exposes students to a wide range of approaches and readings, but also that it provokes reflection upon the distinctiveness (if any) of the discipline that they are studying at undergraduate or postgraduate level: Do disciplinary boundaries make sense, what do they look like, and who—if anyone—is attempting to police them? Hearing students asking those kinds of self-reflective questions about the discipline that they are studying is a satisfying moment for any teacher. They don't happen every week, or with every student, but there are times when it is clear that something they have read has pushed a student to ask bigger questions about doing history and being a historian.

Notes

1. See especially Peter Novick, *The Holocaust in American Life* (Boston: Houghton Mifflin, 1999) chapters 7–9.
2. Terrence Des Pres, "Holocaust Laughter?" in Berel Lang (ed.), *Writing and the Holocaust* (New York: Holmes & Meier, 1988).
3. Saul Friedlander (ed.), *Probing the Limits of Representation: Nazism and the "Final Solution"* (Cambridge, Mass: Harvard University Press, 1992).
4. Novick, *The Holocaust*, uses the phrase "The Years of Transition" for part three of his study.
5. See in particular the exchange between Peter Novick and Lawrence Baron in the pages of the journal *Holocaust and Genocide Studies*. See Lawrence Baron, "The Holocaust and American Public Memory, 1945–1960," *Holocaust and Genocide Studies* 17, 1 (2003) pp. 62–88 and "Letters to the Editor," *Holocaust and Genocide Studies* 18, 2 (2004) pp. 358–75.
6. Edward Lewis Wallant, *The Pawnbroker* (San Diego: Harcourt Brace & Company, 1989), pp. 20–1.
7. Wallant, *Pawnbroker*, p. 258.
8. Wallant, *Pawnbroker*, p. 25.
9. Wallant, *Pawnbroker*, pp. 103–4.
10. Wallant, *Pawnbroker*, p. 211.
11. Wallant, *Pawnbroker*, p. 121.
12. Wallant, *Pawnbroker*, pp. 191–2.
13. Wallant, *Pawnbroker*, pp. 261–2.
14. Tim Cole, *Selling the Holocaust: from Auschwitz to Schindler. How History is Bought, Packaged, and Sold* (New York: Routledge, 2000) pp. 2–3.
15. See the dubbing of 1993 as the "year of the Holocaust" in the United States, with the opening of the United States Holocaust Memorial Museum and Spielberg's *Schindler's List*, Cole, *Selling*, pp. 13–14.
16. Leonard J. Leff, "Hollywood and the Holocaust: Remembering The Pawnbroker," *American Jewish History* 84, 4 (1996) pp. 353–76.
17. Bosley Crowther, "The Pawnbroker," *The New York Times* (21 April, 1965).
18. Wallant, *Pawnbroker*, p. 3.
19. Leff, "Hollywood and the Holocaust" p. 354, notes that, "for the anomic, the proper pronoun is indeed its, not his."
20. Crowther, "The Pawnbroker."
21. Henry Greenspan, "Imagining Survivors: Testimony and the Rise of Holocaust Consciousness" in Hilene Flanzbaum (ed.), *The Americanization of the Holocaust* (Baltimore: John Hopkins University Press, 1999) p. 50.
22. Greenspan, "Imagining Survivors," p. 49
23. Judith E. Doneson, *The Holocaust in American Film* (Syracuse: Syracuse University Press, 2002) p. 8.
24. Doneson, *Holocaust*, p. 9.
25. Crowther, "The Pawnbroker."
26. Malcolm Boyd, "Cycle of Pain," *The Christian Century* (28 July, 1965) p. 943.
27. Wallant, *Pawnbroker*, p. 272.

28. Wallant, *Pawnbroker*, pp. 278–9.
29. This is a point made by Alan Mintz, *Popular Culture and the Shaping of Holocaust Memory in America* (Seattle: University of Washington Press, 2001) pp. 120–4.
30. Crowther, "The Pawnbroker."
31. Ilan Avisar, *Screening the Holocaust: Cinema's Images of the Unimaginable* (Bloomington: Indiana University Press, 1988) p. 124.
32. Hilene Flanzbaum, "'But Wasn't it Terrific?' A Defense of *Life is Beautiful*," *Yale Journal of Criticism* 14, 1 (2001) pp. 273–86.
33. Tim Cole, " 'The Holocaust Industry?': Reflections on a History of the Critique of Holocaust Representation" in Konrad Kwiet & Jürgen Matthäus (eds), *Contemporary Responses to the Holocaust* (Westport: Praeger, 2004) pp. 37–57, esp. pp. 47–9.
34. See especially on this, Charles S. Maier, *The Unmasterable Past. History, Holocaust, and German National Identity* (Cambridge, Mass.: Harvard University Press, 1988).
35. See e.g. James E. Young, "Toward a Received History of the Holocaust," *History and Theory* 36, 4 (1997) pp. 21–43.

11
Sophie's Choice: On the Pedagogical Value of the "Problem Text"
R. Clifton Spargo

Among the most widely read of all Holocaust fictions, William Styron's *Sophie's Choice* (1979) is a risky choice for any course on the Holocaust if only because it has evoked from Jewish critics, much as his previous novel *The Confessions of Nat Turner* did from African-Americans, grave consternation about its justness and accuracy as historical representation. Styron's public statements about the Holocaust, both preceding publication of his novel and after its sensational success, revealed an agenda that, while ostensibly humanitarian, nevertheless relied on a discourse of universalism almost willfully deaf to the cultural territorial issues evoked by such history. As historian Deborah Lipstadt has shown, for a variety of reasons—including strategic focus on the war effort, a scepticism about atrocity stories from the previous world war, and governmentally cued fears about provoking reactionary sentiment in an American public that was strongly anti-immigrant and at least partly anti-Semitic—the American press only minimally covered the Nazi genocide during the war, consistently obscuring reference to the Nazis' central victims, the Jews. When reports of the mass killings did find their way into American newspapers, more often than not Jewish victims were referred to by nationality (as Poles, Czechs, Russians), or mentioned as Jews only alongside Catholics or other Christians who were enduring purportedly similar persecutions. Even liberal organizations friendly to the Jewish refugees avoided mention of Jews as the centrally persecuted people under Hitlerism, so as not to aggravate conservative or utilitarian sentiments against the refugees. Styron's novel, no matter how one reads its temporally layered, convoluted plot, encourages from both Jewish and objectively historicist perspectives some continuation of the dynamic of displaced reference presiding over the initial American response to the Holocaust as well as many subsequent formulations of its significance in United States culture.

I often teach Styron's *Sophie's Choice* because it directly evokes this tendency in American cultural memory to overlook historical specificity for a peculiarly bland understanding in which political oppression is taken as a sign of universal evil. I include the novel in a course I regularly teach on "American Literature and Cultural Memory of the Holocaust," frequently varying my selections from among a vast canon of literary responses to the Holocaust in United States literature, many of which—including works by figures such as Randall Jarrell, Flannery O'Connor, Sylvia Plath, Reynolds Price—are by non-Jewish writers. By placing works about the Holocaust by these non-Jewish writers alongside momentous works of Jewish-American Holocaust literature, by Edward Lewis Wallant, Saul Bellow, Philip Roth, and Cynthia Ozick, I draw students' attention to the pervasive response to the Holocaust in American literature and to the different stages of that response. Indeed, by covering a great many fictional works prior to that era now conventionally designated as predicative of the Holocaust's ascendancy in United States culture (late 1960s to early and mid 1970s), I suggest that the persistence of an imaginative encounter with the Nazi genocide reveals the Holocaust to be peculiarly an American memory and not simply a strangely imported one. Though it did not happen on American soil as did other injustices with which it purportedly competes for our attention, the frequency and fullness of the American imaginative response to the Holocaust indicate something much more than a responsibility imposed by the memory of a minority ethnic group on the general American public.

My choice to include *Sophie's Choice* in a course on American memory of the Holocaust offered at a Jesuit Catholic university is deliberately designed to elicit some of the cultural assumptions and ideological premises that inform the cultural encounter with the Holocaust by non-Jewish, mostly Christianized Americans. In some of the early lessons for the course, I ask students to recall how they first learned about the Holocaust and what elements of their culturally mediated engagement with this particular historical event depend on non-Holocaust related issues. *Sophie's Choice* is a hard text to teach not least because students often prefer it, perhaps for all the wrong reasons, to other harder-hitting American Holocaust novels by authors such as Wallant or Bellow. Over the years my pedagogical design for teaching Styron's novel has become somewhat socratic, in that I allow the students to greet the novel in naiveté and candour, usually with fairly consistent results, foremost of which is a kind of relief: finally, a truly non-Jewish story. I am always a little surprised, even taken aback, by their fondness for *Sophie's Choice*. For a novel that is by any account full of difficult, sometimes overwrought prose to succeed so directly, there must be something else besides literary or entertainment value at work. My contention is that my students' enthusiastic identification with Sophie corresponds all too neatly with popular American reception of the novel and the movie based on it. And all of this has to do with a desire in the common reader to discern only the most overt level of representation precisely because to delve deeper, even in cooperation with the writer's apparent intentions, might take one too close to ideological sources of cultural dissonance. The American public's reading of *Sophie's Choice* has too often declined to consider (and this is true even among certain Jewish critics who have lamented the novel) its representation of anti-Semitism. Nevertheless, I maintain, Styron explicitly framed his novel as a dissonant, rhetorically problematic text, surely meaning for us to stumble on and trouble ourselves over several ideological aspects of the novel. By teaching *Sophie's Choice* as a representative example of the "problem text" of Holocaust literature, I thus hope to open up larger pedagogical questions about how to read, about what we read, and about how we might read against the grain of ideologically determined patterns of identification that in many cases misconstrue the author's own intentions for the work in question.

Sophie's Choice as "problem text"

In adopting the term "problem text" to speak of *Sophie's Choice* I allude deliberately to the category of "problem play," which emerged in the nineteenth century to describe drama that overtly took up social problems, often featuring characters who squared off to present various ways of understanding the specific ill in question—prostitution, venereal disease, or the oppressive everyday influence of the domestic sphere on women. Henrik Ibsen became the name most associated with this provocative mode of drama, and George Bernard Shaw, especially in his early Ibsen-influenced plays such as *Mrs Warren's Profession* (1893), drew the form toward an explicitly socially reformative rhetoric. When F. S. Boas borrowed the term for Shakespeare criticism, it quickly underwent a semantic shift, coming to describe such plays as *Troilus and Cressida*, *The Merchant of Venice*, and *Measure for Measure* in which Shakespeare seemed unable to reach a generically satisfying conclusion. Such formal irresolution may have had something to do with the contents of these plays, since they often addressed specific social issues, but what marked them as especially problematic for early twentieth-century Shakespeare critics was their resistance to the generic work of morally sorting out the good from bad and suggesting by play's end where we ought to line up and with whom. The term "problem play" was useful, then, but not necessarily appreciative. It pointed toward something recalcitrant in the play and its central content, almost as though the Shakespeare text proved inadequate, in its representational reach, to the reality of which it had taken measure. The term also self-referentially alluded to a problem of critical praxis: these were plays that troubled critics by not offering up their insights so readily, by seeming to resist both the clarifying light of reason and the humanist hope of staging our lesser so as to discover our better selves.

I teach *Sophie's Choice* under the rubric of the problem text, overtly introducing the concept of the "problem play." What I do from the very beginning of the unit is teach to the points of controversy. "Teaching the controversy" has become a pedagogical catch-phrase in certain circles, and it can be an artificial exercise, especially if all one intends by it is to illustrate how conflicting hermeneutical procedures (say, Marxist vs. deconstructionist theory) necessarily arrive at different interpretations of the same text. In that fairly uncontroversial sense, every text of literature contains a multitude of meanings and begets, potentially, an interpretive controversy. Some works of literature, however, have provoked controversy as more than a theoretical exercise (in American literature, as Jonathan Arac has fully explored, *The Adventures of Huckleberry Finn* would be paramount of all problem texts). Already by way of our cultural reception of them such texts function as repositories or vehicles of ideological controversy, generating often divisive debate about the meaning of a historical event and its implications. *Sophie's Choice* is a "problem text" in this latter sense.

For early reviewers, *Sophie's Choice* seemed at its best a formally daring and experimental novel, at worst an ungainly mess, for many something of both. It was a ménage of free-associative, apparently irrelevant, quasi-adolescent sexual meditations, of reflections on American (Southern) guilt over slavery and racism, and of a Polish-Catholic survivor's confused remembrances of her homeland and her horrific ordeal under the Nazis; and Styron failed somewhat to make the parts cohere (see Atlas; Aldridge; Symons; Alter). This charge of formal incoherence was a first intimation of the novel's status as problem text. Its rising to the number 1 spot on the *New York Times* bestseller list and thereafter being accounted as a crown jewel of American literature soon made the need to reckon with its problems all the more urgent. In presenting *Sophie's Choice*, I always emphasize the novel's ambitiousness in scale as one possible reason for its seeming incoherence. More importantly, I ask my students to keep in mind the nagging formal concerns raised by early reviewers in case they should prove to be illustrative of the novel's handling of socio-political issues as of the Holocaust itself.

After presenting some of the formal concerns, I begin to help students pursue the controversial ideological dimensions of Styron's representation. By way of introduction, I present the idea that Styron, despite his declared humanitarian interest in the Holocaust, may have courted some of the controversy his novel inspired. By presenting students with a brief synopsis of the cultural reception of *The Confessions of Nat Turner* (1967)—of the hostility the novel generated among many African-American readers and critics, of the defence waged on Styron's behalf by his close friend James Baldwin and also by Ralph Ellison, and of Styron's own expressions of wounded innocence in response to such charges—I suggest that Styron could not have proceeded blindly, yet once more, onto such fraught and ethnically identified territory without some expectation of giving offence. *The Confessions of Nat Turner*, despite or maybe because of the controversy it generated, took the Pulitzer Prize in 1968, not a bad reward for the provocation of controversy. That *Sophie's Choice* courts, if only ironically, the controversy of his 1967 novel is apparent from

Styron's attributing his own thinly veiled literary resumé to Stingo. Stingo, who recounts Sophie's story many years after it occurred, has by the time of this telling become notorious as a consequence of a novel he wrote about slavery, which won him mostly "cranky and insistent" accusations from black people. In response to being termed a "lying writer," who profited from "the miseries of slavery," he has withdrawn into "masochistic resignation." And yet, in representing his younger self (a version of Styron's), Stingo does not hold back on free-associative, vaguely guilty remembrances of Southern youth or on reports of his ambivalence about having profited (most directly, by an inheritance of money made from the sale of a slave by his great-grandfather) from the terrible past of slavery. In short, Styron conspicuously presents Stingo as alter-ego by portraying him as controversial novelist, and as this infamous prehistory presides over the telling of Stingo's/Sophie's story, it solicits our interest by promising to encroach yet once more—as in fact the novel does—on highly taboo imaginative territory.

On the strength of such literary historical data, I typically ask students in one of the early meetings if they can intuit some cause for concern about choices Styron makes in *Sophie's Choice*. In my experience, some free-associative discussion (still relatively unguided by myself at this point) results in students' bringing to the surface the following problems among others: 1) Stingo objectifies women, Sophie included, and the entire novel seems overly sexualized; 2) Stingo and his father are at least vestigially racist; 3) Nathan seems indiscriminately bigoted against Southerners; 4) Nathan is terribly abusive of Sophie; and 5) Nathan, as an American Jew, has no right to claim dominion over the meaning of the Holocaust when, after all, it is Sophie who actually suffered its terror firsthand. All of the first four responses have some validity as readings of the novel and seem largely compatible, at least hypothetically, with Styron's transparent design. Some pretty meaningful conversation about the novel can be generated through such responses, and from closer examination of the textual evidence by which such impressions are arrived at. It is the far more troubling fifth point, however, that has become the center of my own pedagogical response to the novel.

The first time I taught *Sophie's Choice* this last response caught me by surprise, not because I was unaware of it as a potential reading of the novel but because I believed that the way I'd framed the course ought to have prevented such a response. By this point in the semester students had been introduced to the basic facts of and theories about the Holocaust (as of this year I've begun to use Michael Bernard-Donals's *Introduction to Holocaust Studies* to lay much of the historical ground); and they'd also, through the work of historians such as Walter Laqueur, David Wyman, and Deborah Lipstadt, been made aware of the United States's failed response to the European refugee crisis and the role played by anti-immigrant and anti-Semitic attitudes in that failed response. Styron's explicit rhetorical aim of universalizing the lessons of the Holocaust, of warning humanity at large about its capacity for evil, might indeed have turned on his strategic rhetorical displacement of Jewish moral authority. But even if Styron's novel can be understood rhetorically to advocate a displacement of Jewish Holocaust memory, and I think this remains an open question, I was surprised to find my students cooperating with its most overtly troubling ideological gesture. The element of anti-Semitism in *Sophie's Choice* is, however, more difficult to diagnose than is sometimes supposed by Styron's staunchest critics, and this is precisely because the novel represents its own apparent inclinations to anti-Semitism, bringing them to the surface most conspicuously in a series of emotional remarks by Stingo, who as an apparently reliable narrator draws us in to his ideological orb. What we have then, in the truest sense, is a *problematic* mimetic art, the difficulty of which can be measured by its capacity to involve us, perhaps even unwittingly, in its own apparent complicity with persistent, latent ideologies such as anti-Semitism.

Framing the issues: ideology, anti-Semitism, and the memory of victims

The pedagogical approach I am espousing here presumes, and then gradually discovers, a more or less unrecognized impulse in readers of *Sophie's Choice* toward, if not overt anti-Semitism, then at least rivalry of a specifically ideological or ethnically fragmenting kind. The novel constructs, in other words, the need for a privileged centre of moral authority based on cultural paradigms for identity. My goal is to bring students to a recognition of this cultural procedure and its relevance to many of the centrally contested facts of Styron's plot (such as those pertaining to the actual biographical data of Sophie's past, which are explicitly contested within the narrative and not only by way of our exterior discernment). In constructing the "problem" of *Sophie's Choice* along these lines, I do not imagine the novel's meaning to have been exhausted by our perception of its rhetoric of displacement (as too many critics decide). Rather, I insist on treating displacement itself, and associated questions about prejudicial language and social patterns and political structures of oppression, as the matter of this text.

The hermeneutics of displaced memory

I have suggested that my students fairly quickly discern a rivalry between Nathan's self-privileging claim to Holocaust interpretation and Sophie's experience of suffering under the Nazis. A session of free-associative brain-storming, or perhaps a more formal assignment such as the group position-papers I often assign students, may give rise to such insight. In one such position-paper presented on *Sophie's Choice*, my students concluded (I paraphrase loosely):

> Nathan connects himself so strongly with the Holocaust that he pretends he can know what the victims themselves went through. "As a Jew," he says, "I regard myself as an authority on anguish and suffering" (Styron 1979: 71; 1992 Vintage: 75). In this statement, he fails to recognize that it was Sophie who endured "real suffering." Nathan as an American Jew lacks direct experience of the Holocaust and desperately needs to feel a connection to it. He tends to claim his Jewish identity as a form of superiority. By devoting himself to all things that connote the Holocaust, from the Nuremberg Trials to his survivor girlfriend, he connects himself to that which he never experienced.

Lest my students' response seem aberrant, I remind readers that this is almost exactly the paraphrasing of the plot offered by D. G. Myers in his polemic against Styron's novel as a liberal tract denouncing Jewish exclusivists' reign over public memory of the Holocaust (Myers 2001: 508–12). For Myers, the novel's lesson is all too transparent: Jews need to stop thinking of themselves as the only ones who suffered the Holocaust. Myers attacks contemporary left-liberals and especially assimilationist Jews who, by erasing their particularist positionality for the sake of the nation-state, cooperate with insidious forms of anti-Semitism that perform genocide by other means. A synopsis of Myers' position can be used (especially if introduced alongside Paul Breines's rebuttal of Myers in the same issue of *American Literary History*) to establish the genuine controversy Styron's influential rendering of the Holocaust continues to provoke. If one wishes to proceed by way of textual sources for the novel, however, Styron's 1974 *New York Times* essay on a then-recent Holocaust conference, in which he lamented the "narrow view of Nazi totalitarianism" espoused by many Jews, and a 1976 essay by Cynthia Ozick, in which she accused Styron of a historically imprecise humanism, neatly frame the development in *Sophie's Choice* of a rivalry presiding over American Holocaust memory.

Nathan and Sophie are the primary figures for such a rivalry, and Stingo the oddly compromised mediator. Not surprisingly, in response to this plot structure, many critics have interpreted Styron's choice to write about a Polish Catholic survivor as a polemical gesture, a perspective that seems validated by Stingo's rather nakedly competitive rationale in remarking that Sophie had "suffered as much as any Jew who had survived the same afflictions," maybe "more than most" (Styron 1979: 219; 1992 Vintage: 237). Much criticism on the novel, insofar as it engages the core element in this problem text, either condemns the overtly appropriative politics of Styron's take on the Holocaust or apologizes for his right to approach the subject even as non-Jew. To suggest that the choice to tell the story of a non-Jewish Holocaust survivor inherently involves a displacement of the centre of Holocaust memory seems to me grossly simplifying, and some of the controversy about the novel has become mired in such simplifications. As historian Doris Bergen admirably insists, the stories of other victims—Roma (gypsies), homosexuals, Communists and political dissidents, Poles and other devastated ethnic groups—deserve to be told, and we need to hear them to understand the Holocaust in all its dimensions. Too much of our current debate presumes that any story told about other victims necessarily decentres the predominant narrative of the Nazi genocide, which is ineluctably anti-Semitic and focused especially on the Jews. But there is no necessary reason why the aesthetic performance or cultural rehearsal of other Nazi victims' stories cannot be cooperative in the best sense with memory of Jewish victims (as is the case, for instance, in Jorge Semprun's *The Long Voyage*), encouraging us to understand the range and degrees of political persecution.

Useful supplementary texts

Styron, "Auschwitz"; Ozick, "A Liberal's Auschwitz"; Paul Breines, "An Assimilated Jew Speaks"; D. G. Myers, "Jews Without Memory."

Discussion questions

1) Is memory inherently premised on rivalry?
2) Does Styron's strategic relocation of Holocaust memory to a non-Jewish victim perform an ideological act of displacement?
3) Does memory of other victims of Nazism in part or on the whole decentre the genocide against the Jews?

The cultural procedures of anti-Semitism

Styron cannot be easily folded back into a cooperative or even analogical understanding of oppression, and it seems to me that a proper reading of the novel must acknowledge the contentiousness in his privileging of Sophie. Where that contentiousness becomes most evident is in his demonization (perhaps more accurately daemonization) of Nathan Landau, Sophie's American Jewish saviour, lover, and tormenter. As the portrait of Nathan develops, he comes to stand for Styron's rivalry with American-Jewish fiction writers (in the novel Nathan pronounces the emergence of an American-Jewish literati with which Stingo must contend) and with those who claim ownership of the Holocaust, and his assistance and persecution of the novel's real Holocaust victim stands allegorically for the hypocrisy of American Jews who would claim the Holocaust as their own experience. The progress of Nathan's statements in this direction and Stingo's resistance to them can be readily charted, and I try to get students to see that what seems most inordinate in Nathan's accusations against Sophie and Stingo pertains to his allegorical function, as he stands for Jewish outrage. In this context I have found it sometimes helpful to introduce Holocaust survivor Jean Amery's "Resentments," in which resentful outrage, conducted in the name of memory, is espoused as a moral position. Nathan cannot be fully recuperated to sympathy within the narrative, but his inordinate outrage can be viewed as partaking of a symbolic register, as though he were pronouncing a historical *j'accuse* against not only Germany and Poland but also the United States. Amery speaks as a victim of persecution and torture, but also for victims and for the meaning of their experience in culture. I use his essay to push students to overturn their narrow view of testimony and suffering as strictly experiential toward an ethical, ideological, and political understanding of how the mere facts of genocide and of a collectively victimized people challenge our conventional understanding of culture and morality.

My point, then, is not to exonerate Nathan from the fictional facts of his presentation, but to ask students to inquire into the ideological stakes of his apparent demonization and to wonder whether seeing him more as daemon (the outraged spirit of a historical moment) than demon alters Styron's narrative logic in any way. In the course of this discussion, I try to get students to examine their as-yet undiscerned but nevertheless culturally determined reasons for embracing this storyline, in which a non-Jewish, relatively atypical Holocaust survivor is victimized by a non-survivor American Jew. My goal here is not to elicit a confession of unacknowledged anti-Semitism. To seek such confessions in the classroom would be as ideologically contrived and historically falsifying as it would be pedagogically coercive (as such, it would recall the simplified politics of morality exploited, for example, on an episode of the deeply conservative television show *Seventh Heaven* in which a Holocaust-denying parent accidentally listens to a Holocaust survivor tell her story and then weeps repentantly over the error in his ways). Similarly, I do not try to corner Styron's novel between alternately condemning scenarios of incoherence and insidious anti-Semitism. Ideology, particularly the peculiar ideological lure of anti-Semitism, does not yield itself to sudden light and easy clarity. It is that which we have to work to perceive, especially insofar as we are implicated in it. American anti-Semitism is not now what it was once, and neither in 2006 nor, say, 1943 was it in any way interchangeable with Nazi anti-Semitism, but that does not mean our society does not abide, often in subtle ways, by cultural codes and narratives that preserve anti-Semitism.

What I try finally to elicit is a recognition of the extent to which the novel compulsively repeats and yet recasts debates about anti-Semitism. For instance, I introduce students to the interpretive practice of supersessionism that for so long dominated most major strains of Christian theology, according to which Jewish covenantal privilege was understood to be narrow, legalistic, and finally obsolete when viewed, retrospectively, by way of the new covenant. I show them how the stereotype of the Jew as bound by law (developed foundationally by Paul's epistles) is of a piece with such a hermeneutics, casting the Jew always in the defensive position of literalist or particularist or self-centred parochialist. Considering how the representation of Nathan conforms to some of these prejudicial representational patterns, we inquire, with specific reference to the overtly anti-Semitic language deployed in the novel, whether Styron's text makes apparent its own or Stingo's complicity in that habit of thought.

Newly attuned to the novel's immersion in anti-Semitic language, I return them to an examination of the presiding rivalry—Nathan versus Sophie/Stingo—to see how the Jewish versus Christian paradigm is implicit in it. Literary reading, I suggest, still most often turns, for both better and worse, on a suspension of disbelief so active as to persuade us that we know villainy when we see it, that we've rightly sympathized with the text's central victim or protagonist and not with the one who persecutes her. Yet, I ask them, is this the only way to read a novel or this novel specifically? Should we read distrustfully? Or, might we discern a mimetic dimension of art that by reproducing the fact and even affect of prejudice, can involve a self-reflective or ironic dimension according to which the manifest meanings of the plot (those perceived, say, by Stingo) are subtly betrayed? Our dilemma, I suggest, constitutes an almost perfect parallel to the structure of identification presiding over Shakespeare's own infamously ambiguous document of anti-Semitism, *The Merchant of Venice*. By way of this literary historical analogy, I suggest that our orchestrated identification with one character as the virtuous or martyrologically pure principle in a text (Portia or Sophie) may be a complementary function of a text's exploitation of prejudice. With reference to Portia's eager repression of Shylock's Jewishness at the end of *The Merchant of Venice*, I chart Sophie's concealment of her anti-Semitic familial history, suggesting the ways in which her strategic concealment mirrors the structure of storytelling in the novel, which perpetuates itself on the strength of the untold or not yet revealed underlying plot. Sophie's self-preserving, anti-Semitic sentiments in the camps (she professes herself an anti-Semite to curry favor with the commandant) suggest a complexly layered story of ideology, in which the truth of what she believed or what she did in the past will not emerge easily. By briefly introducing students (via John Gross and James Shapiro) to the stage history of *The Merchant of*

Venice and to post-Holocaust productions of it, which tended overwhelmingly to portray Shylock sympathetically, I make them consider the difficulty involved in any aesthetic text representing prejudice. The more apparent the author's disenchantment with prejudice is in the text itself, the less persuasive, and so less urgent, the represented prejudice may seem. In light of this, I ask, how much of Stingo's anti-Semitic language and the novel's apparently anti-Judaic plot should we ascribe to the author's ideological complicity with anti-Semitism, and how much to the mimetic praxis of reproducing it for our examination?

Useful supplementary texts
Shakespeare, *The Merchant of Venice*.

Discussion questions
1) Is Nathan fundamentally a realistic or allegorical character?
2) Is Nathan demonized as a consequence of psychological motives in Stingo we can or ought to be able to perceive?
3) When Sophie courts favour with the commandant by claiming co-authorship of her Polish father's anti-Semitic pamphlets, ought we to understand this false confession as tracing any truth? Are her father's sins also hers or merely his own?

The politics of resentment: victims and injustice
Styron's representation of victims and the aftermath of victimization is troubling on several fronts, and I believe these questions need to be confronted straight on. Elaborating my own published hypothesis that the "memory of injustice" is constitutive of any postmodernly connoted ethics while also frankly admitting my own suspicion of a great deal of cultural language about the victim (Spargo 2006, esp. 120–38), I ask students to consider how the rivalry set up between Nathan as Jew and Sophie as persecuted Pole suggests, fundamentally, a distrust of the victim. Having previously discussed Nathan in conjunction with Amery's plaintive revaluation of Nietzschean ressentiment, I encourage their deeper analysis of Styron/Stingo's presentation of Sophie as newly paradigmatic victim. In a 1980 interview, Styron explained that in characterizing Sophie he wanted to be sure she was not "just a pathetic victim" (see Mills 1985), and in this regard he was merely echoing a line from the novel itself ("If Sophie

had been just a victim . . . she would have seemed merely pathetic" [Styron 1979: 219; 1992 Vintage: 237]). What such language suggests at a deeper level is Styron's own culturally determined mistrust of the victim, even the fictional victim he has preferred to other claimants (such as Nathan) of victim status. This distrust, expressed by Styron as by Stingo, greatly troubles the presumption of identification on which students have typically based their own rejection of Nathan, for it suggests how deeply contradictory many of Styron's ideas about victimization are. On this note, I introduce feminist criticisms of the novel, developing an interpretation that would make Styron a critic of the social victimization of women against one in which the novel seems highly complicitous with oppressive ideological constructs of women (see Durham 1984; Carstens 2001). Sophie is at once deeply pathologized (drawn, as a kind of inveterate victim, to Nathan's persecuting love) and relentlessly cast as eroticized object, even in her most severe moments of degradation. Her history of repeated sexual assault could, in the best sense, be understood to encode our further investigation of a woman's sexual exploitation, but it might also, in a much less encouraging light, be a sign of voyeuristic prurience. Lisa Carstens's insistence that the novel renders Sophie's memory as confessional rather than testimonial, thus implicitly characterizing her as her responsible for the fate she suffered, is a provocative feminist reading of the novel that seems, in large part, hard to refute. Still, I've found it useful to introduce Primo Levi's "Shame" as an ethically compelling argument on behalf of what psychoanalysts, with pathological emphasis, had once deemed "survivor's guilt." I ask my students whether Sophie's guilt is by the terms of Styron's representation pathological or ethical, and how we would begin to decide this question.

Two final, interrelated themes round out my discussion of the victim: resentment, and shame. The first is a consideration of the portraiture of perpetrators in the novel. Styron's fictional renderings of the historical figures Hans Frank, Nazi Governor General of Poland, and Rudolf Höss, commandant of Auschwitz, and his purely fictional invention of SS doctor Jemand von Niemand have contributed to the critical resistance to his novel among scholars of the Holocaust (see Rosenfeld 1980: 161–3). Especially in the portrait of von Niemand, who we are told inflicts pain out of some quasi-existentialist desire to commit a "totally unpardonable sin," the novel encourages an imaginative identification that seems to involve a misplaced (or displaced) compassion. Not only might this portrait seem offensive to the memory of Holocaust victims, but it also provides a rationale for representing Sophie as complicitous in her own fate. Through discussion of the controversy over Hannah Arendt's representation of Eichmann and a brief turn to the terms of Levi's "The Gray Zone," we discuss the question of whether the intimation of increased culpability of the victim correlates with mitigation of the perpetrators' responsibility for events.

Oddly, Styron seems more willing to consider the possibility of dishonest victims than of lying perpetrators, and it is on this note that I open up the final—more generally philosophical—theme of our reading: how historical truth is embedded in testimony. Drawing together much of what we've already discussed, I ask students to consider the layered unreliability of narration in the novel—our reasons for distrusting what we learn from Nathan, our reasons for distrusting what we learn from Sophie, and our reasons for distrusting what we learn from the apparently reliable narrator Stingo (not least of which are his vestigial racism, his conspicuous objectification of women, and his occasional anti-Semitism). Returning to the question of Sophie's lies (on this subject, see also Durham 1984: 456–63), I chart for the students the dramatic structure of the narrative as the discovery of three major secrets: 1) Nathan's insanity; 2) Sophie's anti-Semitic past; and 3) Sophie's being forced to choose between her two children—which one will live, which will die.

To the extent that Sophie's familial anti-Semitism is interwoven with the deep secret of her personal loss, the novel puts us in a very difficult place, properly akin to what Levi called "the gray zone." And in this sense secrecy and its active complement, lying, provide much of the impetus for the novel's method of storytelling, which is focused intensively on gradual recovery of truths pertaining to the most awful and historically overdetermined personal history. Getting beyond lies and the painful secrets they conceal is the hermeneutical method of the novel, but once we are there, where exactly have we arrived? Are we brought to historical or merely personal truth, and how is the spectre of ideology operative in such fictional, mock-testimonial truth?

Useful supplementary texts

Jean Amery, "Resentments"; Hannah Arendt, *Eichmann in Jerusalem*; Primo Levi, "Shame" and "The Gray Zone."

Discussion questions

1) To what extent does Styron present Nathan as a plausible spokesperson on behalf of the historical reality of Jewish victimization in the Holocaust?
2) Is Styron generally mistrustful of the victim's experience? Is this evident in his characterization of Sophie?
3) What use does Styron make of analogies between victims' experiences? In invoking Stingo's awkward negotiations with his Southern identity and memory of slavery, what analogies does Styron draw between Stingo (and the "racist" American South) and Sophie (and "anti-Semitic" Poland)?
4) How should a novelist represent a perpetrator? What is the line between understanding and forgiveness? Does Styron's portrait of Dr Niemand effectively rationalize the Nazi doctor's crimes?

Works cited

Aldridge, John W. *Harper's Magazine*, Sept. 1979, 97.
Alter, Robert, *Saturday Review*, 7 July 1979, 43.
Amery, Jean, "Resentments," *At the Mind's Limits: Contemplations by a Survivor On Auschwitz and Its Realities*, trans. Sidney Rosenfeld and Stella P. Rosenfeld (Bloomington, IN: Indiana University Press, 1980).
Arac, Jonathan, *Huckleberry Finn As Idol and Target: the Function of Criticism in Our Time* (Madison, WI; University of Wisconsin Press, 1997).
Arendt, Hannah, *Eichmann in Jerusalem: a Report on the Banality of Evil* (New York: Viking Press, 1963).
Atlas, James W., *New York Times Book Review*, 27 May 1979, 18.
Bergen, Doris, *War and Genocide: a Concise History of the Holocaust* (Lanham: Rowman and Littlefield, 2003).
Bernard-Donals, Michael, *An Introduction to Holocaust Studies* (Upper Saddle River, NJ: Prentice Hall, 2006).
Breines, Paul, "An Assimilated Jew Speaks: Notes on 'Jews Without Memory,'" *American Literary History* 13 (Fall 2001), 530–9.
Carstens, Lisa, "Sexual Politics and Confessional Testimony in *Sophie's Choice*," *Twentieth-Century Literature* 47.3 (Fall 2001), 293–324.
Durham, Carolyn A., "William Styron's *Sophie's Choice*: the Structure of Oppression," *Twentieth Century Literature* 30: 4 (Winter 1984), 448–64.
Gross, John J., *Shylock: Four Hundred Years in the Life of a Legend* (London: Chatto & Windus, 1992).

Levi, Primo, "The Gray Zone" and "Shame," *The Drowned and the Saved*, trans. Raymond Rosenthal (New York: Summit Books, 1988).

Lipstadt, Deborah, *Beyond Belief: the American Press and the Coming of the Holocaust, 1933–1945* (New York: Free Press, 1986).

Mills, Hilary, "Creators on Creating: William Styron," *Conversations with William Styron*, ed. James L. W. West III, trans. W. Pierre Jacoebee (Jackson, MI: University of Mississippi Press, 1985), 217–33.

Myers, D. G., "Jews without Memory: *Sophie's Choice* and the Ideology of Liberal Anti-Judaism," *American Literary History* 13 (Fall 2001), 499–529.

Ozick, Cynthia, "A Liberal's Auschwitz," *The Puschcart Prize: Best of the Small Presses*, Vol. 1, ed. Bill Henderson (Yonkers: Pushcart, 1976), 149–53.

Rosenfeld, Alvin H., *A Double Dying: Reflections on Holocaust Literature* (Bloomington: Indiana University Press, 1980).

Shapiro, James, *Shakespeare and the Jews* (New York: Columbia University Press, 1996).

Spargo, R. Clifton, *Vigilant Memory: Emmanuel Levinas, the Holocaust, and the Unjust Death* (Baltimore: Johns Hopkins University Press, 2006).

Styron, William, *Sophie's Choice* (New York: Random House, 1979); paperback reprint (New York: Vintage International, 1992).

———. "Auschwitz," *This Quiet Dust and Other Writings* (New York: Random House, 1982), 303–4.

Symons, Julian, *Times Literary Supplement*, 30 Nov. 1979, 77.

The Holocaust: Historical, Literary, and Cinematic Timeline

(Note: Books and films are cited in the following formats: Books: Author, *Title*; Films: *Title* (Director, Country). For non-English language texts in all cases the standard English title has been used.)

1933 *January 30*: Nazis take power
March 9: concentration camp established at Dachau, outside Munich
April 1: state-sponsored boycott of Jewish shops and businesses
1935 *May 21*: Jews forbidden to serve in the German armed forces
September 15: promulgation of Nuremberg Laws
1936 *June 17*: Reichsführer SS Heinrich Himmler appointed head of all German police and security services
1938 *March 12*: Anschluss [union] of Austria; Austrian Jews immediately deprived of civil rights, subjected to Nazi race laws; by September, all Viennese Jewish businesses (33,000 in March) liquidated
May: concentration camp established in the granite quarries at Mauthausen, near Linz (Hitler's birthplace)
June 9: main synagogue in Munich burnt down by Nazi stormtroopers
July–September: Jews forbidden to practice law or medicine
October 6: Italy enacts anti-Semitic racial laws; 27: 18,000 Polish-born Jews deported to Poland
November 10: Kristallnacht; 191 synagogues fired; 91 Jews murdered; over 30,000 arrested; 20% of all Jewish property levied confiscated to pay for damage; *12*: Göring orders the liquidation of all Jewish businesses by year's end; *15*: Jewish children banned from German schools
December: no Jewish-owned businesses (of over 6,000 in 1933) remain in Berlin
(Kathrine) Kressmann Taylor's 'Address Unknown', published in *Story* Magazine
1939 *January 30*: in his annual speech commemorating the Nazi seizure of power, Hitler predicts that a new world war will result in "the annihilation of the Jewish race in Europe"
March 15: Partition of Czechoslovakia: 118,000 more Jews fall under German dominion
September 1: Germany invades Poland (Jewish population in 1939: approx. 3.5 million); 5,000 civilian Jews murdered before the end of October; *3*: France and Britain declare war on Germany: start of World War II

	November 12: Jews expelled to the "General Government" (occupied Poland) from Polish areas incorporated into Greater Germany; 28: decree to establish Jewish Councils in all Polish Jewish communities December 11: all Jews in the General Government made liable to two years' (minimum) forced labour
1940	February 8: Lodz Ghetto established April–June: concentration camp (Auschwitz I) established in former army barracks at Oswiecim [Auschwitz], near Cracow October 3: Warsaw Ghetto established November 28: Anti-Semitic propaganda film *Der Ewige Jude* (*The Eternal Jew*, Fritz Hippler) premieres in Berlin
1941	January: Two thousand people a month are dying of starvation in the Warsaw Ghetto; 13: start of deportations of "work battalions" from the Lodz Ghetto to Chelmno June 22: "Operation Barbarossa"—Germany invades the USSR; German forces are specifically directed that Geneva conventions do not apply to Jews and Communists; within five weeks, more Jews killed by mobile *Einsatzgrüppen* and regular army units than in previous 8 years of Nazi rule July 31: Göring, on Hitler's behalf, directs Heydrich with finding "a complete solution to the Jewish question" September 3: 600 Soviet POWs gassed using Zyklon B at Auschwitz Camp I September 27–28: 34,000 Russian Jews machine-gunned to death at Babi Yar ravine, near Kiev October: deportations of Jews from Germany, Austria, Czechoslovakia, to Polish ghettoes begin October 23–24: 35,000 Jews shot or burned alive in Odessa; 27–30: some 600 Jewish elderly in Kalisz, western Poland, killed by carbon monoxide gas November 24: Ghetto established at Theresienstadt, Czechoslovakia (the "paradise ghetto") December 1: *Einsatzkommando* 3 reports that only 15% of Lithuanian Jews remain alive (34,000 of 234,000 in 1939); 7: gassing vans begin operation at Chelmno [Kulmhof]: at least 360,000 Jews killed by end 1942
1942	January 20: Wannsee conference to determine operational responsibility for "final solution of the Jewish question" February: "Operation Reinhard" extermination camps established at Belzec, Treblinka, Sobibor; first gassings of Jews using Zyklon B at Auschwitz-Birkenau March: gassings begin at Belzec; of 600,000 Jews deported by December 1942, only 2 survive April: construction begins of extermination camp at Auschwitz-Birkenau; operations commence at Sobibor: 250,000 dead by December, 64 survivors

	July: Treblinka operational: up to 850,000 dead by August 1943; around 80 survivors at war's end
1943	*April 18*: Warsaw Ghetto uprising begins; by the final liquidation of the ghetto in May, 7,000 Jews killed in combat, 30,000 deported to Treblinka
	August 2: 150 worker Jews (of 750) escape in uprising at Treblinka; camp later demolished
	October 13: 300 worker Jews (of 600) escape in uprising at Sobibor; camp closed
1944	*March*: deportation of Hungarian Jews to Auschwitz begins
	July 8: Hungarian deportations halted at insistence of Hungarian authorities under international pressure; 437,000 Jews have been deported to Auschwitz
1945	*January 18*: evacuation of Auschwitz begins; "death marches" to Germany; *27*: Russian troops enter Auschwitz
	April 2: a survivor of the Sobibor revolt murdered by anti-Semitic Poles; *15*: British troops enter Belsen; *29*: American troops enter Dachau; *30*: Hitler commits suicide in his Berlin bunker: in his political testament, he blames the Jews as the "guilty party" in the war
	May 8: Germany surrenders to the Allies
	May–June: over 350 Jews are killed in anti-Semitic incidents in Poland
1946	Trial of leading Nazis at Nuremberg; 12 hanged for war crimes and crimes against humanity
1947	Primo Levi, *If This Is a Man* first edition published: poor sales
	Olga Lengyel, *Five Chimneys*
1948	*The Last Stage* (Wanda Jakubowska, Pol)
	Border Street (Aleksander Ford, Pol)
1951	Hannah Arendt, *The Origins of Totalitarianism* (first edition)
1953	Publication of *The Diary of Anne Frank*
1955	*Night and Fog* (Alain Resnais, Fr)
1958	Elie Wiesel, *Night*
1959	André Schwartz-Bart, *The Last of the Just* wins Prix Goncourt
1960	Adolf Eichmann abducted from Buenos Aires by Mossad agents; tried in Jerusalem and executed for crimes against the Jewish people
	The Diary of Anne Frank (George Stevens, US)
1961	Raul Hilberg, *The Destruction of the European Jews*
	Kitty Hart, *I Am Alive*
1963	Hannah Arendt, *Eichmann in Jerusalem*
	Jorge Semprun *Le Grand Voyage* (*The Long Voyage*)
1963–65	Trial of 21 Auschwitz SS officers in Frankfurt-am-Main
1964	Rolf Hochhuth, *The Deputy*
1965	Hannah Arendt, *Eichmann in Jerusalem: A Report on the Banality of Evil*
	The Pawnbroker (Sidney Lumet, US)
1966	Jean-François Steiner, *Treblinka* is a controversial bestseller in France

	Jean Améry *Jenseits Von Schuld Und Sühne* (*At the Mind's Limits*)
	Peter Weiss, *The Investigation*
1969	Jurek Becker, *Jacob the Liar*
	The Sorrow and the Pity (Marcel Ophuls, Fr)
1973	Gitta Sereny, *Into That Darkness*
1974	*Jacob the Liar* (Frank Beyer, GDR)
1976	Tadeusz Borowski, *This Way for the Gas, Ladies and Gentlemen*
	Imre Kertész, *Sorstalanság* (*Fatelessness*)
1978	*Holocaust* mini-series broadcast on NBC (US); subsequent broadcast in West Germany provokes major shift in prevailing attitudes towards the Holocaust
1979	William Styron, *Sophie's Choice*
1981	D. M. Thomas, *The White Hotel*
	Kitty Hart *Return to Auschwitz*
1982	*Sophie's Choice* (Alan J. Pakula, US)
	Thomas Kenneally, *Schindler's List* (UK: *Schindler's Ark*)
1985	*Shoah* (Claude Lanzmann, Fr)
1986	Art Spiegelman, *Maus: a Survivor's Tale*
	Primo Levi, *The Drowned and the Saved*
	War and Remembrance mini-series broadcast on ABC (US)
	Elie Wiesel awarded Nobel Peace Prize
1991	Martin Amis, *Time's Arrow*
	Cynthia Ozick, *The Shawl*
	Art Spiegelman, *Maus II: "And Now My Troubles Really Began"*
	Europa, Europa (Agnieszka Holland, Fr/Pol)
1993	*Schindler's List* (Steven Spielberg, US): "Best Picture", "Best Director", "Best Adapted Screenplay" and 4 other Academy Awards
	US Holocaust Memorial Museum opens
1994	*Don't Touch My Holocaust* (Asher Tlalim, Israel)
	Jorge Semprun, *L'écriture ou la vie* (*Literature or Life*)
1996	Binjamin Wilkomirski, *Fragments: Memories of a Childhood, 1939–1948*
	Daniel Goldhagen, *Hitler's Willing Executioners: Ordinary Germans and the Holocaust* is a highly controversial international bestseller
1997	Anne Michaels, *Fugitive Pieces*
1998	*Life is Beautiful* (Roberto Benigni, It): "Best Original Screenplay" Academy Award
	Wladislaw Szpilman, *The Pianist*
	Wilkomirski's *Fragments* exposed as fake
2000	Holocaust denier David Irving loses libel claim against Penguin Books
	Imperial War Museum opens permanent Holocaust exhibition
2001	*Amen* (Costa-Gavras, Fr/Germ)
2002	*The Grey Zone* (Tim Blake Nelson, US)
	Uprising (Jon Avnet, US)
	The Pianist (Roman Polanski, US-Fr): "Best Director", "Best Actor" Academy Awards
	Jonathan Safran Foer, *Everything is Illuminated*

	Holocaust survivor and Novelist Imre Kertesz wins Nobel Prize for Literature
2005	*Fateless* (Lajos Koltai, Hungary)
2006	Anthony Littell, *Les Bienveillantes* [*The Kindly Ones*] wins Prix Goncourt

Further Reading

Avisar, Ilan, *Screening the Holocaust: Cinema's Images of the Unimaginable* (Bloomington: Indiana University Press, 1988).
  The second (after Insdorf, see below) dedicated study of this field. More selective and hence in-depth than Insdorf, it also lacks real engagement with theoretical debates.
Banner, Gillian, *Holocaust Literature: Schulz, Levi, Spiegelman and the Memory of the Offence* (London: Valentine Mitchell, 2000).
  A good account of these three writers, with a tight focus.
Bartov, Omer, *Mirrors of Destruction: War, Genocide and Modern Identity* (Oxford: Oxford University Press, 2000).
  A wide-ranging account of the aftermath of the Holocaust in a range of areas, with some fascinating complex ideas. Very good on the relationship between literature and history.
——. *The "Jew" in Cinema: From* The Golem *to* Don't Touch My Holocaust (Bloomington: Indiana University Press, 2005).
  A subtle, probing and often illuminating discussion of a wide variety of European, American, and global films.
Berger, James, *After the End: Representations of the Post-apocalypse* (London: University of Minnesota Press, 1999).
  While not specifically on the Holocaust, much of this densely argued book deals with Holocaust representation in contemporary literature and theory.
Bernstein, Michael André, *Foregone Conclusions: Against Apocalyptic History* (London: University of California Press, 1994).
  A forcefully argued and timely book, which, by focusing on the ways in which Holocaust texts are "backshadowed" by our knowledge of the events, aims to help us read these texts in more radical ways.
Caruth, Cathy (ed.) *Trauma: Experience and Memory* (London: Johns Hopkins University Press, 1995).
——. *Unclaimed Experience: Trauma, Narrative and History* (London: John Hopkins University Press, 1996).
  These two texts make up a key part of the intellectual core of Trauma theory: they are closely argued and complex works, drawing on philosophy and literary theory, and have been very influential in the field.
Clendinnen, Inga, *Reading the Holocaust* (Cambridge: Cambridge University Press, 1999).
  Rather overrated series of mediations on the history of the Holocaust, with little sense of the literary.
Cole, Tim, *Images of the Holocaust: the Myth of the "Shoah" Business* (London: Duckworth, 1999) (US Title: *Selling the Holocaust. From Auschwitz to Schindler. How History is Bought, Packaged, and Sold* (1999)).

Excellent, closely-argued case-study based account of the historical construction of Holocaust memory: focuses on Anne Frank, Adolf Eichmann, Oskar Schindler, Auschwitz, Yad Vashem, and the US Holocaust Memorial Museum.

Delbo, Charlotte, *Aucun de nous reviendra* (Paris: Editions de Minuit, 1970).

Des Pres, Terence, *The Survivor* (London: Oxford University Press, 1976).

Perhaps the first book of "Holocaust Criticism." Many of the terms and ideas it explores in Holocaust testimony (the will to bear witness, excremental assault, nightmare, and waking and others) are central. Highly recommended.

Doneson, Judith E., *The Holocaust and American Film*, 2nd edn. (New York: Syracuse University Press, 2002).

Important analysis of the ways in which American cinema has struggled to incorporate the Holocaust into its dominant narrative paradigms.

Duras, Marguerite, *La Douleur* (Paris: POL, 1985).

Eaglestone, Robert, *The Holocaust and the Postmodern* (Oxford: Oxford University Press, 2004).

Wide-ranging account that covers literature, testimony, historiography, philosophy. It shows how postmodern thought stems from a reflection on the Holocaust, and how, in turn, this illuminates many issues in Holocaust studies. Focuses on testimony, second generation memory, contemporary literature, the philosophy of history (including the Goldhagen/Browning debates, Holocaust Denial and the work of Saul Friedlander), Emmanuel Levinas, Jacques Derrida, and the question of the Human.

Falconer, Rachel, *Hell in Contemporary Literature* (Edinburgh: Edinburgh University Press, 2005).

The Holocaust, with second generation memory, forms the core of this outstanding book. Very useful and innovative.

Felman, Shoshana and Laub, Dori, *Testimony: Crises of Witnessing in Literature, Psychoanalysis and History* (London: Routledge, 1992).

A very important intervention in theory and Holocaust debates. Made up of seven essays on interlinked issues, and drawing on psychoanalysis and on literary theory, the book poses an array of complex and demanding questions around the idea of trauma and of witnessing.

Flanzbaum, Hilene (ed.) *The Americanisation of the Holocaust* (London: Johns Hopkins University Press, 1999).

An insightful and timely collection of essays on a range of topics germane to the title.

Foley, Barbara, "Fact, Fiction, Fascism: Testimony and Mimesis in Holocaust Narrative," *Comparative Literature* 34 (1982), 330–60.

One of the earliest pieces of "Holocaust Criticism," this article lays out a range of ideas that have since become central to the field.

Friedländer, Saul (ed.) *Probing the Limits of Representation: Nazism and the "Final Solution"* (Cambridge, Ma.: Harvard University Press, 1992).

This ground-breaking collection of historical and historiographical studies has had a huge impact on the field of Holocaust studies. As a book that opens up questions, rather than provides answers, it disturbs more than it concludes.

Haggith, Toby, and Newman, Joanna (eds), *Holocaust and the Moving Image: Representations in Film and Television since 1933* (London: Wallflower, 2005).
A rather uneven anthology of essays, though usefully combining contributions from filmmakers alongside standard academic essays.

Hartman, Geoffrey (ed.), *Holocaust Remembrance: the Shapes of Memory* (Oxford: Blackwell, 1994).
A far-reaching and demanding collection of essays and reflections.

———. *The Longest Shadow: in the Aftermath of the Holocaust* (Basingstoke: Palgrave Macmillan, 2002).
Geoffrey Hartman is one of the world's leading critics, intellectually sensitive and insightful. This collection of his writings on the Holocaust is full of moments of terrible clarity, subtle argument and powerful ideas. Highly recommended.

Heinemann, M. E., *Gender and Destiny: Women Writers and the Holocaust* (Westport: Greenwood Press, 1986).
One of the first accounts to focus on issues of gender in relation to representing the Holocaust.

Hirsch, Joshua, *Afterimage: Film, Trauma, and the Holocaust* (Philadelphia: Temple University Press, 2004).
Heavily weighted like so many others towards *Shoah*, this is nonetheless one of the most sophisticated critical interventions in this field to date.

Hirsch, Marianne, *Family Frames: Photographs, Narrative and Postmemory* (London: Harvard University Press, 1997).
It is in this book that Hirsch coins the term "Postmemory" in her discussion of second generation testimony.

Horowitz, Sara, *Voicing the Void: Muteness and Memory in Holocaust Fiction* (New York: State University of New York Press, 1997).

Hungerford, Amy, *The Holocaust of Texts* (London: University of Chicago Press, 2003).

Huyssen, Andreas, *After the Great Divide* (London: Macmillan, 1986).
A startling collection of essays, ranging across media and focusing on German memory.

Insdorf, Annette, *Indelible Shadows: Film and the Holocaust*, 3rd edn. (Cambridge: Cambridge University Press, 2003).
Pioneering and indubitably comprehensive survey of Holocaust films, but the critical analysis is by contemporary standards very lightweight.

King, Nicola, (2000) *Memory, Narrative, Identity: Remembering the Self* (Edinburgh University Press).
A well-formed account of the relation of memory and identity and their manifestation in and through textuality.

LaCapra, Dominick, *History and Memory after Auschwitz* (Ithaca, NY: Cornell University Press, 1998).

———. *Representing the Holocaust: History, Theory, Trauma* (Ithaca, NY: Cornell University Press, 1994).

All of LaCapra's work engages with the Holocaust in complex and detailed ways. Unflinching, the work draws on a wide and heterogeneous range of intellectual sources to confront issues of trauma and representation, and of the philosophy of history. Highly recommended.

Lang, Berel, *The Future of the Holocaust: Between History and Memory* (London: Cornell University Press, 1999).

———. and Gigliotti, Simone, *The Holocaust: a Reader* (Oxford: Blackwell, 2004).

All of Lang's serious and dense work, stemming from analytic philosophy, is worth reading, though his conclusions are often controversial.

Langer, Lawrence, *The Holocaust and the Literary Imagination* (New Haven: Yale University Press, 1975).

———. Langer, Lawrence, *Holocaust Testimony: the Ruins of Memory* (London: Yale University Press, 1991).

Ground-breaking account of the impact of video-testimony, which has set the terms of debate in this area since its publication.

———. (ed.), *Art from the Ashes: a Holocaust Anthology* (Oxford: Oxford University Press, 1995).

Very full anthology of primary sources and some historical work.

———. *Pre-empting the Holocaust* (New Haven: Yale University Press, 1998).

Langer is one of the world's leading scholars in this field (beginning with *The Holocaust and the Literary Imagination*). His work is deeply serious and very well-informed. Although it has not responded in detail to more contemporary critical and theoretical concerns, it lays the groundwork for much in Holocaust studies and this book can be seen as summing up many years of thought and research.

Lipstadt, Deborah, *Denying the Holocaust* (London: Penguin, 1993).

The first and most celebrated of many books about Holocaust denial: it works by exploring detailed case studies.

Maechler, Stefan, *The Wilkomirski Affair* (London: Picador, 2001).

Including the text of the false memoir *Fragments*, this is nearly all one needs to know about the Wilkomirski affair.

Novick, Peter, *The Holocaust and Collective Memory* (London: Bloomsbury, 1999).

This widely celebrated account covers the "History of the History of the Holocaust" in a highly informed and lucid way. Very focused on the US, it makes a cogent and controversial argument about the reasons of interest in the Holocaust.

Paizis, George and Leak, Andrew (eds), *The Holocaust and the Text* (London: Macmillan, 2000).

Interesting and widely-focused collection of essays from a range of disciplines. Particular highlights include Anna Hardman's essay "Representations of the Holocaust in Women's Testimony" and Bryan Cheyette on George Steiner's post-Holocaust fiction.

Perec, Georges, *W ou le souvenir d'enfance* (Paris: Denoël, 1975).

Reiter, Andrea, *Narrating the Holocaust*, trans. Patrick Camiler (London: Continuum, 2000).

A very detailed and comprehensive survey of the field, with a lot of data drawn from an extensive corpus of survivor literature. Recommended.

Rothberg, Michael, *Traumatic Realism: the Demands of Holocaust Representation* (Minneapolis: University of Minnesota Press, 2000).

    An excellent recent intervention in the field. Closely argued, it makes the case for a mode of representation that is neither realist, modernist, nor postmodern, but "traumatic realism." The book covers theorists and philosophers as well as testimony and literary texts.

——. and Levi, Neil, *The Holocaust: Theoretical Readings* (Edinburgh: Edinburgh University Press, 2003).

    An excellent reader with a wide range of well-selected excerpts from primary and secondary sources. Currently, the best teaching and textbook resource for a Holocaust course.

Rowland, Antony, *Tony Harrison and the Holocaust* (Liverpool: Liverpool University Press, 2001).

——. *Holocaust Poetry: Awkward Poetics in the Work of Sylvia Plath, Geoffrey Hill, Tony Harrison and Ted Hughes* (Edinburgh: Edinburgh University Press, 2005).

    Both these excellent books—the first more focused, the second with a broader remit—cover the ways in which post-Holocaust Anglophone poetry have taken up the Holocaust. Rowland explores what he names "awkward poetics" in these writers, and argues that it is an integral response to the events of the Holocaust.

Schlant, Ernestine, *The Language of Silence* (London: Routledge, 1999).

    A full study of a range of German writers responding to the Holocaust.

Schwartz, Daniel, *Imagining the Holocaust* (Basingstoke: Palgrave—now Palgrave Macmillan, 1999).

    A survey of major texts in the field.

Shandler, Jeffrey, *While America Watches: Televising the Holocaust* (New York: Oxford University Press, 1999).

    Enormously well-researched and wide-ranging, pathbreaking discussion, informed by contemporary scholarship and critical debates in television studies.

Sicher, Efraim, *The Holocaust Novel* (London: Routledge, 2005).

    An up-to-date survey of the "Holocaust novel," which here includes testimony as well as more recent work by writers who are not survivors. A very useful overview.

Steiner, George, *Language and Silence* (New York: Athenaum, 1967).

    One of the first major "theoretical" engagements with the issues.

Todorov, Tzvetan, *Facing the Extreme* (New York: Henry Holt, 1996).

    Rather overrated account of a range of Holocaust texts.

Vice, Sue, *Holocaust Fiction* (London: Routledge, 2000).

——. *Children writing the Holocaust* (Basingstoke: Palgrave Macmillan, 2004).

    Sue Vice's work is characterized by a width of knowledge and profound sense of the issues involved. *Holocaust Fiction* covers a range of texts which have been controversial, and explores them and the reasons for controversy.

Children writing the Holocaust looks at the significance of the ways in which different view points construct the Holocaust.

———. (ed.) *Representing the Holocaust* (London: Vallentine Mitchell, 2003).

A wide-ranging collection of essays, covering film, literature and historiography.

Whitehead, Anne, *Trauma's Fiction* (Edinburgh: Edinburgh University Press, 2004).

Wiesel, Elie, "The Holocaust as Literary Inspiration" in *Dimensions of the Holocaust* (Evanston: Northwestern University Press, 1990).

This is a seminal essay by one of the most significant survivors.

Young, James, *Writing and Rewriting the Holocaust* (Bloomington: Indiana University Press, 1990).

James Young's first book, *Writing and Rewriting the Holocaust*, changed the shape of the literary study of the Holocaust. Involved in theory, and with a very wide range of reference, it is a vital contribution to the field and very highly recommended. If literary/theoretical debates have developed since its publication in 1988, they have done so on the terms set by this book. The later book is an in-depth study of Holocaust memorials, that, in this more restricted field, too has set the terms of discussion.

———. *The Texture of Memory: Holocaust Memorials and Meaning* (London: Yale University Press, 1993).

Zelizer, Barbie (ed.) *Visual Culture and the Holocaust* (London: Athlone, 2001).

Excellent selection of essays on a wide range of visual culture, including art, television and film, architecture, photographs, the net, and the body. Demanding and thoughtful.

For more information/resources on teaching English (both print and web-based) please go to the following link on the English Subject Centre website: www.english.heacademy.ac.uk/explore/resources/scholarship/publication. php

Index

Adorno, Theodor   5, 8, 10, 29, 30, 34, 54, 55, 58, 65, 66, 67, 87
Agamben, Giorgio   14, 106
Amen   64, 73
Amery, Jean   148, 154
Amis, Martin   6, 51, 56, 58, 61
Amistad   38, 43, 45
Antelme, Robert   30, 54, 96
Apocalypse Now   113, 123
Appelfeld, Aharon   51, 59
Appignanesi, Lisa   7, 51
Arac, Jonathan   142
Arendt, Hannah   8, 153, 154
Asscher-Pinkhoff, Clara   32
Audiard, Jacques   105
Auschwitz   64
Auschwitz, Auschwitz-Birkenau   21, 22, 24, 34, 39, 45, 49, 54, 58, 63, 94, 108, 120, 121

Bakhtin, Mikhail   9, 24
Baldwin, James   143
Barthes, Roland   32
Bauman, Zygmunt   8
Bellow, Saul   140, 141
Belsen   49
Belzec   22
Benigni, Roberto   18, 71, 126
Benjamin, Walter   35
Bergen, Doris   147
Berger, Peter   31
Bernard-Donals, Michael   16–18, 53
Bernstein, Michael Andre   59
Bersani, Leo   107
Beth Shalom   8
Blake, William   115
Blanchot, Maurice   8, 30
Boas, F. S.   142
Bomba, Abraham   69, 110

Borowski, Tadeusz   7, 21, 22, 23, 71, 84, 87
Breines, Paul   147, 148
Brookner, Anita   7
Browning, Christopher   8, 33, 34
Butler, Judith   23

Camus, Albert   3
Carr, E. H.   80
Carter, Angela   123
Caruth, Cathy   8, 30, 39, 53, 57
Casablanca   71
Caviani, Lilian   49, 72
Cayrol, Jean   107, 108
Celan, Paul   3, 7, 24, 25, 51, 54, 87
Chelmno   109
Cixous, Hélène   23
Clinton, Bill   43
Cole, Tim   33, 42
Coleridge, Samuel Taylor   39, 116
Conrad, Joseph   116
Crowther, Bosley   135

Dachau   22, 96
Dante   12, 114, 115, 116, 118–20, 122
Dawidowicz, Lucy   21
de Beauvoir, Simone   93
Dean, Carolyn,   86
Delbo, Charlotte   7, 11, 23, 38–41, 93, 94
Derrida, Jacques   8
des Pres, Terence   8, 30, 49, 71, 127
Didi-Huberman, Georges   106, 108
Divided We Fall   72
Doneson, Judith   103, 133
Dostoevsky, Fyodor   3
Duras, Marguerite   93, 96
Dutoit, Ulysse   107

Index

Eaglestone, Robert 56, 59, 60, 78, 81, 82, 85
Eichmann Trail 127
Eisler, Hans 107
Eliot, T. S. 116, 123
Ellison, Ralph 143

Fackenheim, Emil 8, 9, 34
Falconer, Rachel 31, 51
Farrell, Kirby 31
Felman, Shoshona 3, 4, 8, 12, 14, 17, 18, 30, 31, 55, 102, 103, 111
Figes, Eva 7
Fink, Ida 8, 22
Flanzbaum, Hilene 135
Foer, Jonathan Safran 8
Foley, Barbara 58, 59
Foucault, Michel 9, 32
Frank, Anne 7, 45, 49, 51, 60
Frank, Hans 152
Freud, Sigmund 3, 34
Friedlander, Saul 107, 127

Gandersheim 96
Gengis Cohen 64, 72
Gershon, Karen, 32
Gigliotti, Simone 28
Gilroy, Paul 31
Ginsberg, Terri 103
Glejzer, Richard 16–18, 53
Goddard, Jean-Luc 12, 106
Goebbels, Joseph 61
Goldhagen, Daniel 81
Gothic Literature 54
Gray, Alasdair 114, 123
Greenspan, Henry 132
Grey Zone, The 64, 73
Grynberg, Henryk 32

Halbwachs, Maurice 42
Harris, Robert 6, 7, 10, 57, 58, 59
Hartmann, Geoffrey 1, 14, 28
Hegel, G. W. F 34
Hilberg, Raul 8, 34, 69, 75, 81

Hill, Geoffrey 6, 8, 24, 87, 88
Himmler, Heinrich 57, 61
Hirsch, Joshua 108
Hirsch, Marianne 37, 46, 85, 95, 111
Historkestreit 136
Hitler, Adolf 58
Holocaust 64, 66, 70, 73, 75
Horowitz, Sara 50, 52, 53, 55, 56
Höss, Rudolf 152
Hungerford, Amy 31
Huyssen, Andreas 71

Ibsen, Henrik 142
Ilsa, She-wolf of the SS 72, 73
Intentional Fallacy 32
Irigaray, Luce 23

Jarrell, Randall 140

Kacanades, Irene 46, 85, 95
Kaplan, E. Ann 31
Karpf, Anne 51
Kenneally, Thomas 55
Kertesz, Imre 6
King, Nicola, 29
Krantz, Charles 107

LaCapra, Dominick 3, 8, 33, 41, 46, 61, 68, 110, 111
Lang, Berel 28, 29, 33, 52, 107
Langer, Lawrence 8, 17, 29, 30, 53, 57, 58, 93
Lanzmann, Claude 10, 25, 38, 39, 41, 51, 68, 70, 91, 93, 103, 105, 106, 109, 110, 111, 126
Laqueur, Walter 145
Laub, Dori 4, 30, 31
Leff, Leonard 130
Lejeune, Philippe 53
Levi, Neil 8, 28
Levi, Primo 6, 7, 9, 12, 22, 23, 38, 39, 49, 50, 51, 53, 55, 61, 82, 96, 97, 114–23, 152, 153
Levinas, Emmanuel 8, 35, 74, 87

Life is Beautiful 18, 19, 64, 66, 71, 126, 127
Lindbergh, Charles 59
Lipstadt, Deborah 139, 145
Littell, Jonathan 11
Luckhurst, Roger 87
Lumet, Sidney 126
Lyotard, Jean-François 1, 8, 57

Majdanek 108
Malle, Louis 105
Marker, Chris 104
Marrus, Michael 8
Marx, Karl 34
Michaels, Anne 6, 51, 54, 55
Middle Passage 43, 44
Mihailenu, Radu 105
Milgram, Stanley 33
Millu, Liana 23
Milton, John 115, 120, 123
Moll, James 107, 108
Morrison, Toni 38, 44
Myers, D. G. 146

Nalkowska, Zofia 7
Nancy, Jean-Luc 106
Nasty Girl, The 64
Nazis: a Warning from History, The 8, 64, 67
Nietzsche, Friedrich 34
Night and Fog 6, 19, 64, 65, 67, 69, 70, 74, 82, 100, 103, 105, 106, 111
Nomberg-Prztyk, Sara 7
Nora, Pierre 42
Novick, Peter 8, 20, 42, 128

O'Connor, Flannery 140
Ophuls, Marcel 105
Ozick, Cynthia 7, 52, 140, 148

Pawnbroker, The 126–36
Perec, George 6, 7, 11, 49, 50, 51, 53, 93, 96
Pianist, The 64, 75
Plath, Sylvia 8, 140
Prager, Emily 51, 58, 60

Price, Reynolds 140
Psycho 71

Radnoti, Miklós 24
Rancière, Jacques 106
Ravensbruck 94
Reading, Peter 114
Rees, Lawrence 22
Resnais, Alain 12, 19, 100, 103–5, 108, 111
Ricoeur, Paul 95
Roma 147
Roots 71
Rose, Gillian 2, 67, 88, 106
Rosen, Norma 50
Ross, Benjamin 73
Roth, Philip 59, 140, 141
Rothberg, Michael 8, 28, 31, 37, 111
Rousso, Henry 91
Rushdie, Salman 123

Sachs, Nelly 51
Sartre, Jean-Paul 92
Schindler's List 6, 19, 38, 40, 43, 45, 49, 51, 54, 58, 70, 66, 73, 74, 75, 80, 85, 111
Schlink, Bernhard 51, 61
Schwartz, Daniel 30
Sebald, W. G. 7, 38, 41, 61
Semprun, Jorge 6, 7, 92–5, 97, 98, 99, 147
Shakespeare, William 150
Shaw, George Bernard 142
Sheppard, Robert 84
Sherman, Martin 22
Shoah 6, 38, 39, 40, 51, 64, 65, 66, 68, 70, 71, 73, 74, 75, 93, 100, 103, 105, 106, 126 109–11, 126, 127
Six Day War 127
Speer, Albert 58
Speigelman, Art 7, 22, 38, 44, 51, 80, 126
Spielberg, Steven 10, 19, 38, 40, 43, 50, 51, 55, 68, 70, 71, 110
Srebnik, Simon 69, 109

Stangl, Franz 74
Steiner, George 9, 50, 67
Stéphane Mallarmé 3
Stewart, Victoria 48, 53
Stonewall 22
Styron, William 6, 13, 140–7
Suleiman, Susan Rubin 96, 98, 99

Tal, Kali 31
Tavernier, Bertrand 105
Tel Aviv 110
Toderov, Tzvetan 111, 116
Torgovnivk, Mariana 31
Torte Bluma 73, 74
Train of Life 64, 72
Treblinka 22, 69, 110

Uprising 64
US Holocaust Memorial Museum 8, 38, 42, 43

Valman, Nadia 29
Varda, Agnes 104
Vice, Sue 1, 8, 9, 29, 31

Vichy France 92
Vichy Syndrome 91
Virgil 115, 122

Wallant, Edward Lewis 126, 140, 141
War and Remembrance 64
Warsaw Ghetto Uprising 63, 64, 85
Weissman, Gary 111
White, Hayden 34
Whitehead, Anne 31, 57
Wiesel, Elie 6, 7, 9, 22, 29, 43, 50, 51, 62, 100
Wilkomirski, Binjamin 7, 56, 126
Wilson, Emma 108
World at War, The 8, 64, 67, 68
Wyman, David 145

Young, James 8, 29, 30, 31, 35, 42, 44, 52, 55, 57, 59, 95

Žižek, Slavoj 105